A Funny Little Story
About the Death of My Mother

A Funny Little Story About the Death of My Mother

Jan Nash

Copyright © 2009 by Jan Nash

All rights reserved. No part of this publication may be reproduced or transmitted in any form or by any means, electronic or mechanical, without permission in writing from the author.

Cover Photo by Jan Nash

For Abe.
Jewell would have liked you.

WHY?

I didn't set out to write a book about my mother dying. I'm a fairly happy-go-lucky person so, if I was going to choose a topic for a book, I'd choose something happy-go-lucky. You know, "Everything You Always Wanted to Know about Rainbows" or "Tie-Dye: The First Fifty Years." I would not choose to write about cancer. But, then again, my mother didn't choose to have cancer either. Sometimes, you just have to work with what life gives you.

Actually, I didn't set out to write a book at all. I was just driving northbound on the 405 about six months after my mother's diagnosis and a voice in my head said, "Write a book." I pay attention to voices in my head (unless they say something like "Run naked down the produce aisle") because I believe God guides me using these random, little moments. I get good ideas for stories, answers to difficult problems and, often, life-changing instructions. And, if some other events or people reinforce one of these strange ideas, I really sit up and take notice. So, a week later when my cancer-stricken mother, Jewell, asked me, "Are you writing all this stuff down so you can write a book?" I took it as a sign and I started keeping a "cancer" journal. Everything that follows is based on the notes I made while Jewell was sick.

* * * * * *

I have kept a journal for most of my adult life. Typically, I'd write a page or two every now and then, about one hundred handwritten pages a year. At twenty lines a page, ten words a line, it's about 20,000 words a year. During the fourteen months of my mother's illness, I wrote one hundred and twenty-five single-spaced typed pages. 56, 283 words. I know that's right because I used the "count" feature on my word processor.

I wrote and wrote and wrote. I couldn't stop myself. I would sit for hours with a notebook or in front of the computer: writing down how my mother told me she was feeling; trying to remember the exact words she's used to express herself; capturing the infinitesimal shifts in her mood and my mood. Writing. As much and as often as I could.

A couple of months after my mother died, I read all 56, 283 words of my "cancer journal." I felt I needed to relive Jewell's experience before I could start the book the little voice told me to write. And, much to my surprise, all of those disconnected entries had a theme: fear. Fear of cancer.

Fear of dying. Fear of being late for airplanes. Fear of talking about feelings. Fear of not talking about feelings. Fear about how I would deal with my mother's death. Fear of how my father would deal with my mother's death. Fear of my mother's suffering. Fear of failing my mother. Fear of bodily fluids. Fear, pure and simple, of almost everything. We were a nice bunch of people wrestling with the difference between our expectations of how life should be and the reality of how it was.

I couldn't figure out how to put all of that fear into some sort of meaningful context until I came across another journal entry written about six weeks before Jewell got sick, before cancer and a concrete fear of death entered our lives.

> Journal, September 27 -- I think about my parents dying and I get sad. I don't feel like I'm being a good daughter, but I don't really know how to be a better one... Someday, probably not too far in the future... they will die. And my chance to let them know they matter to me will be gone. They will exist like Ron exists or Granny Nash. A mental image that begins to lose its sharpness and then the image blurs and then, one day, it is almost invisible...
>
> What is the essence of what we do for each other? What binds us together? What is God trying to teach us?

Finding this entry was like another little voice inside my head. During the fourteen months of my mother's illness, it was as I struggled with my fear that I discovered the answers to those three questions. Fear had been my teacher. This book is about where it led me.

* * * * * *

During one of our daily telephone conversations, my mother told me she thought that cancer had been good for us. It had made us "better people. We're a better family." She asked me what I'd learned from the experience. "Well," I responded. "I think I'm more honest and more in touch with my feelings. Those are good things, I guess… But wouldn't it have been easier if we'd been able to learn all that playing backgammon?" At that moment, like so many others during her illness, my mother laughed. Like I hope she's laughing now.

Journal, November 16 -- My mother was diagnosed with ovarian cancer almost two weeks ago, but today was the day it hit me. It didn't hit me when she called a week ago Thursday and said, "It's bad. I have ovarian cancer." And it didn't hit me when she had to be drained of the ascites fluid again or was scheduled for her surgery or yesterday when I flew down with my sister to visit her. It hit me today, when she begged my father not to make her drink any more "GoLightly," the horribly named fluid that cleaned out her bowels for surgery.

She was supposed to drink four liters [a little over ten cans of soda], eight ounces every fifteen minutes. The first hour passed. She didn't crap and she didn't complain. Thirty-two ounces down. The second hour passed. The crapping started and she became profoundly nauseous. She went to the toilet with a bucket. Green fluid flying out of every orifice. For a while, she could be coerced to continue with funny stories and light persuasion. But then it reached a crossover point. She felt too horrible. And as she walked back to the bed, she began to cry. "Please don't make me drink anymore. Please. I can't drink anymore." My father sat down next to her and he leaned over and rested his head on her shoulder. She lay on the bed crying. "Please don't make me drink anymore."

I walked away. I couldn't watch her desperation or his helplessness. I couldn't bear to think that this might get worse before it got better. I couldn't bear to be reminded that my mother, my lovely mother who just wanted everyone to like her, might die.

Ultimately, she drank all but twenty-four ounces. She refused to go on. And we didn't make her. Who wanted to be responsible for more suffering?

I was getting ready for bed. Brushing my teeth. And, for a moment, wished that I'd led a less spiritual life. Because, if I didn't know God, tonight I could make one of those bargains you see in the movies. "God, if you'll save my Mom, I'll do anything." And maybe it would happen. If I didn't know God, maybe saving my lost soul would be enough to prompt God to help my mother. But I know that God doesn't work that way.

Tomorrow, Jewell will have surgery. And the world will change again. Please God, let it change for the better.

EVERYTHING CHANGES

I was sick on the day the space shuttle Challenger exploded. I hadn't planned to watch the launch, but I was home and all the networks were covering it, so I tuned in. All day long, over and over again, they played that moment: a white smoke trail framed against the bright blue sky suddenly separates into a "Y," two paths where only one was supposed to be. It was horrifying and disorienting. I kept watching, thinking that eventually the image on the screen would make sense. It never did.

My mother's experience with cancer is like that for me, as well. Moments, painful confusing moments, are seared into my brain and replay like news clips, right behind my eyes. Nothing I do, at least nothing I've been able to do yet, can stop them.

* * * * * *

Jewell's cancer snuck up on me. One day, she called and casually informed me that she had some discomfort in her abdomen and was having some "tests." I remember asking what they were testing for and my mom told me that it could be a lot of things, but they were focusing on her liver. A few days, several blood tests and a CT scan later, the doctors had narrowed it down to hepatitis, cirrhosis of the liver and cancer. "What," I asked her, "am I supposed to root for?"

Two weeks later, she called again. It was early in the afternoon. I was at work on "Hiller and Diller," a short-lived ABC sitcom. I took Jewell's call in my office. The room was dark, with just a little bit of late afternoon sunlight streaming in from a high window. I didn't turn on the lights. I just walked behind my desk and, still standing, picked up the beige telephone. I stared at my white sneakers as I twirled a pencil on the top of the desk. I know all these things because the moment is fused in my cortex, as is the following brief conversation. "Hey, what did the doctor say?" I asked my mother. "It's bad," she answered. "I have ovarian cancer."

After that, it all blurs. I know my mother told me she was having surgery, because I went home and made flight arrangements, but I don't remember her telling me when her surgery was, or anything about the disease or how she was doing or how my father was doing. The only other thing I remember is that she said she was sorry. "Mom, you don't have to apologize. You didn't do anything." A heavy pause hung in the air, and then she whispered, "I'm still sorry."

* * * * * *

My mother was the sun around which my family, and her larger extended family, rotated. I do not intend that to be a hyperbolic statement about my mother's importance to us. My mother <u>was</u> the sun around which my family rotated. She was responsible for everything. She planned parties. She organized family events. She remembered birthdays and bought gifts. She told us what to do and when to do it. Yes, she was a little bossy and often a pain-in-the-ass, but every family needs an organizer and Jewell was ours. It made life easy. Nothing ever got forgotten. Cakes were baked. Communion dresses were sewed. Pieces of wood from the farm of beloved grandparents were saved and turned into furniture (no, I'm not kidding). Jewell made shit happen.

Stuff like cancer wasn't supposed to happen to Jewell.

* * * * * *

The news that she did have cancer made me feel powerless. I guess that is the nature of bad news. It leaves you feeling out of control. It is not a feeling I enjoy. I like control. I like order. I even like rules. You know, guidelines to help me get through the day: do unto others as I would have them do unto me; save a little something for a "rainy day"; and make sure to eat a good breakfast. They are tricks for keeping chaos at bay.

But on the day of Jewell's diagnosis, chaos came rushing in, despite the fact that I'd eaten a delicious peanut butter and jelly sandwich for breakfast that morning. It was like the twin plumes of the Challenger smoke trails. My mother having cancer didn't make sense. So, I tried to make it make sense. I started doing something that overly educated people often do... research. Until that day, I don't think I'd spent more than an hour or two on the Internet. I thought it was a sinkhole, lots of people having less interesting personal interactions than they could have if they just went to an auto supply store. It may be that, but it is also a great resource. I found pages and pages of information on ovarian cancer, virtually all of it bad. The main thing I learned is that ovarian cancer is an easy cancer to treat with very high survival rates. If you catch it early... which almost no one does. As a result, lots of the women who are diagnosed with ovarian cancer die.

Jewell didn't catch it early. The only concrete sign her cancer gave her was that she felt bloated, a common symptom in advanced ovarian cancer cases. But, as someone whose weight has fluctuated a lot over her life, she attributed the bloating to fat, not cancer. She cut down on sweets. It didn't help and, one day, she realized she was short of breath. She went to see her doctor and he said she had ascites, a build-up of fluid in her abdominal cavity. He ran some tests. Days passed. He ran a few more tests. After a couple more days, the accumulating fluid made it difficult for Jewell to breathe. So, the doctor decided to drain her to reduce the pressure on her lungs. He stuck a long hollow needle into her abdomen, not unlike sticking a straw into a water balloon; except, unlike a water balloon, my mother didn't burst. Her body just kept pumping ice-tea colored liquid, with little bits of biological matter floating in it, through a hose and into a medical collection bag. Finally, the pressure on her abdomen was reduced enough to turn the flood of ascites into a trickle. My mother had produced her first, official biohazard.

The doctor sent a sample of the fluid to a lab for tests and then sent my mother to the hospital for a spiral CT scan. My parents were early for their appointment, so my father, John, a stubborn guy who likes to fight with "the man," went to the front office to resolve a billing dispute with the hospital. While he was gone, a technician came and pulled my mother aside. "Mrs. Nash, I don't usually do this," he said. "But the lab just called... You don't need to have this procedure. They got back the results on your ascites fluid. You have ovarian cancer. I'm sorry."

My mother, all alone in a waiting room, sat down and cried. Two people came in and, noticing that she was blowing her nose, one turned to the other and said, "Let's not sit here. We don't want to catch her cold."

My normally polite mother snapped. "I have cancer. You can't catch it," she said, and then she blew her nose toward them for emphasis.

THE SURGERY

I spent the week before my mother's surgery preparing. I reviewed treatment options and downloaded charts about drug trials and combination therapy responsiveness. I bought books on alternative cancer treatment, nutrition, chemotherapy, and the role of the mind in the treatment of disease. I even bought meditation tapes. By the end of the week, I had a mountain of stuff. I read it all. I mailed the books and tapes to my mother. I censored the Internet information and e-mailed the upbeat material to my father. I did everything I could do without operating on her myself. I was ready for my mother's survival.

* * * * * *

The morning of my mother's surgery, the "Golightly" disaster behind us, we got ready to go to the hospital. Jewell put on a bright blue cotton sweat suit and white Keds sneakers. We packed her suitcase. And then, as we headed out of my parents bedroom, my mother sat down in a chair by the door. "I meant to show you some things in the house," she said. "In case... anything happens."

"Nothing is going to happen," I replied. "Well... if it does. I want your father to remarry. But his new wife shouldn't get my stuff. I want you girls to get my stuff." Smiling, I assured her that "Julie and I will keep the new wife from getting your stuff." Jewell sat quietly for a moment and then said, "I just don't know how this happened."

* * * * * *

I had this friend, Ron. He had AIDS. He'd been sick for awhile, in and out of the hospital a bunch of times. In the spring, he was hospitalized again, so I went to see him at Cedars Sinai. His speech was slurred. Apparently, he had some sort of lesion on his brain that affected his ability to articulate his thoughts, but he was smiling and gracious, just as he'd been when he'd been healthy. I stayed with him awhile, told him about movies I'd seen, things that had happened at work, people we knew in common. After about an hour, I got up, kissed him, and told him I'd talk to him soon.

Another friend, Dave, was also staying at Cedars Sinai that day. Dave had cystic fibrosis and, as a result of various lung and breathing conditions, had been in and out of the hospital almost as much as Ron. He needed a lung transplant and if he didn't get one, eventually he would die.

Dave looked terrible. He was thin. His eyes were sinking into their sockets. He barely had enough breath for talking. Every word was a struggle. At one point, he started to cough. Deep hacking coughs that sounded like they came from the bottom of his feet. He reached over and grabbed a tube off the wall and started breathing into it. I have no idea what that tube did, but after a minute he stopped coughing and seemed a little more comfortable. The whole fit exhausted him, so I said goodbye and left.

About two weeks later, Ron died, Dave got new lungs, and a few days after that, I was driving to a movie in Hollywood when I came upon an auto accident. A single car, smashed up in the middle of an intersection, a body on the street covered by yellow plastic. Some guy was just driving down the street, thinking about changing the station on his radio and, the next moment, he was dead.

* * * * * *

My mother, her hands pressed tightly in her lap, sat quietly as I told these stories. "It's trite," I said. "But life is weird. Ron dies. Dave lives. The guy in the car was fine one minute and then, suddenly, he wasn't. You've got cancer. That sucks. You didn't step out on the road and get hit by a bus. You've still got a chance." I kissed her and asked if she was ready to go. "No," she answered. "Will you go anyway?" "I guess so," she said. "I'm dressed." So, my mother, my father, my sister, Julie, and I got in the car and drove to the hospital.

SMILE

From the moment Jewell told me that she was sick, I became obsessed with documenting her condition. In the pre-op area that morning, I took a lot of pictures. I have a picture of my mom in her slit-up-the-ass green hospital gown. Of my father standing next to my mother in her gown. Of my sister and me with my mother in her gown. I have a picture of my mother with the woman who took her blood pressure, with the woman who shaved her for surgery, and with the woman who gave her the shot to knock her out. I have a lot of unflattering pictures from that day. And not once did my mother say, "Enough." Every time I pointed the camera at her, she smiled.

When all of the pre-op procedures were done, a nurse came to take her away. It was a weird moment, because as much as we all tried to act normal, this wasn't normal. They were taking my mother away to cut her open and remove hundreds of tiny tumors from her body.

My sister leaned over and whispered something to her. My father and I stood back so Julie could have a moment. After she stepped away, I walked over to the gurney and leaned in towards Jewell. "I'll see you later," I said, as if saying it would guarantee that it was true. "I love you," my mother responded. And then she looked me in the eyes and said, "You're everything I always dreamed you would be."

* * * * * *

I was a perfect child. Like every kid, I was given to occasional bouts of willfulness, intransigence and, often, downright stupidity, but generally I embodied the qualities that my parents were looking for in a youngster. I was happy. I was polite. I didn't have to be prodded to do my homework or strive for success. I respected rules and, even better, so feared getting into trouble; I created rules of my own to follow. I knew how to sit quietly when sitting quietly was required, but I could also engage in pleasant conversation on any number of children's topics if it was not. I was fun, athletic and sociable. I had lots of interests and lots of friends. I dreamed of playing shortstop for the Chicago Cubs. I was, in a word, presentable.

If time had stopped on my eighteenth birthday, it might have been easy for me to believe my mother as they wheeled her away. But time didn't stop, which left me a lot of opportunities to create heartache.

* * * * * *

Except for one slightly wicked week when I was sixteen, I never rebelled against the guidelines my parents and society set for my life while I lived at home. I didn't drink. I didn't smoke (okay, I smoked at a seventh grade party once, but I didn't like it). I didn't run around. So, when I arrived at college and was given unlimited access to alcohol, I promptly lost my mind. Somehow, I managed to get good grades while still drinking my body weight in beer, rum and screwdrivers.

I drank all the time and had the profoundly bad judgment that goes with too much alcohol. I once got drunk with a classmate while sitting on the roof of our dormitory. We drank rum and cokes until the cokes ran out, and then we drank straight rum. I was completely blitzed when I decided to walk across the red tiled roof to climb through a window that opened onto a flight of stairs. I remember the window. I do not remember the stairs or passing out on the bathroom floor or the day and a half of unconsciousness that followed. It is a thirty-six hour period lost to me forever.

I don't think my parents knew how much I drank, but I think they knew something was wrong with me. I wrote letters home that my sister described as "scary." Jewell and John never said anything, but during the Christmas break of my sophomore year when I told them I wanted to drop out of school for a year and travel around the world, they didn't raise any protest. I think they knew that college wasn't working for me, at least at that point in time.

I drank for one simple reason: I wasn't happy. I didn't know I was unhappy at the time. I probably wouldn't know now, except my best friend from college told me that when I was drunk I used to come into her dorm room and pace back and forth for hours, crying and spewing out anger and upset. Alcohol allowed me to vent something I couldn't feel when sober. It was an ineffective way to get in touch with my feelings, however, because the next day I never remembered anything. Years later, I was able to figure out that all of the qualities that made me such a happy and eager-to-please child made me a happy and eager-to-please adult. In a child, it's delightful. In an adult, it's a tad co-dependent.

* * * * * *

A friend used to call me the "Coke Lady." She said that if there were a party, I would take it upon myself to make sure that everyone at the party was having a good time. If someone was alone, I talked to them. If they didn't know people, I introduced them. If they needed a Coke, I got them one. This was my role in life. I got people Cokes. I couldn't help it. I felt better about myself when I was taking care of others. Other people's feelings were more important than my own and I couldn't stand it if anyone was unhappy.

I got it from my family. John, Jewell, Julie and I had our own special brand of dysfunction. As a group, we were really good with positive emotions and really bad with negative ones. If you needed a hug, you were going to get it, but if you were mad at someone, you didn't tell them, not if your very life depended upon it. Usually, you just suppressed it and it would bubble to the surface in some unintended way.

For instance, my mom would be mad at my dad for not fixing the doorbell. Julie and I could tell she was mad, because she kept checking the doorbell to see if it was fixed. It would have been very easy for her to say, "John, I'm very upset you haven't fixed the doorbell." He probably would have gone right then and fixed it. But, instead of doing that, she stewed. All day long she'd think about how he hadn't fixed the doorbell and, then, when he accidentally dropped a paper clip on the dining table, she'd scream, "I just polished that table. Look what you've done. You've ruined the gloss." John would look at her, confused. Then, somewhat sheepishly, he'd pick up the paper clip, wipe the table with his shirt and scurry off to another room.

If someone had a really big problem -- like my mother was hurt that I didn't do anything for Mothers' Day -- they still wouldn't confront the offending party directly. My mother would talk to my father. My father would talk to my sister. And Julie might, if she thought the problem was big enough, talk to me. I wouldn't call my mother to talk to her about what my father had talked to my sister about, but I might call my sister later to follow up and she, in turn, might call my father or my mother to tell them what I said.

The important thing to remember is that, no one ever confronted anyone directly with something painful. We smiled. As dysfunctions go, it's not a horrible one, but it is a little emotionally stunted. Life is full of unpleasant things. It might be nice to deal with them directly. Instead, I emerged into adulthood engaged in a bout of unrelenting, and often completely false, optimism: a smile at any costs.

* * * * * *

I stayed that way until I moved to Los Angeles when I was thirty years old to take a job with The Walt Disney Company. I worked in the company's strategic planning department. I planned things strategically, which as far as I could tell meant that I ran the same bit of analysis over and over again, creating reams of paper than needed constant reformatting. Apparently, the formatting was the most important part, because it was the only thing anyone ever commented on. The job wasn't what I'd hoped, but I met some really nice people while doing it, including a woman named Lauren, who sat in the office across from mine. Lauren hated adjusting the margins on her presentations as much as I hated adjusting the ones on mine. All that mutual complaining made us fast friends. We started carpooling.

We would drive and talk about Strategic Planning, and Lauren would share things from her life. I didn't share. I wasn't a sharer. One day, she asked me how I felt about a particularly unpleasant encounter we had had at the office. I thought about it a moment and then said, "I don't know." Puzzled, she asked, "Don't know, meaning it's really complicated or...?" The truth was, I just didn't know. Negative emotions didn't exist for me. I didn't have access to anger or sadness or irritation. I didn't feel them; I didn't express them. I had spent my whole life ignoring them and making environments "nice."

Lauren found this void hard to imagine. She told me to run through a list of feelings and see if anything triggered a sensation in the pit of my stomach. So, at fifty-five miles an hour headed southbound in the slow lane of the 405, I tried to figure out how I felt. We drove in silence. As we pulled off at the Sunset Boulevard exit, I said, "hurt." I felt hurt.

* * * * * *

It was like math. Now, as an adult, the idea that two plus two equals four is instinctual. I've been adding my whole life. But what was it like that first day as I sat in my tiny desk, giant pencil clutched in my pudgy hand, trying to understand as Mrs. Bassett explained addition? Two numbers get added together and produce a different number? What's up with that? It seems easy now, but, as a first grader, I must have felt like my head was exploding. Feelings were like that for me, too. I didn't know I wasn't having negative feelings. Or, put more accurately, that I was having them and not acknowledging them. Two plus two equals four? First your head explodes. And then you realize you're hurt.

* * * * * *

Learning how to have feelings transformed my life. Suddenly, I had all sorts of feelings. Not just good ones, but bad ones, and bad ones that led to good ones, and good ones that led to bad ones, and bad ones that led to worse ones that led to horrible ones. It was incredible.

And then one day, I had a feeling that was neither good nor bad. It just was. I realized I was gay.

Of course, I was gay before that moment. I just could never face that gnawing feeling in the pit of my stomach. It was too scary. But one day, after thinking about it quietly for a long time, I said it out loud, if obliquely. I was standing in a grocery store line, buying oranges and reading the "National Enquirer." On the cover was an article about some celebrity whose sexuality was in dispute. "You know, if sexuality is a spectrum," I said to Lauren. "I think I'm more gay than you are." "How gay are you?" She asked. "I don't know," I responded.

Suddenly, having said the words out loud, they lost some of their power to frighten me. I didn't want to be gay, but if I was, I needed to be honest about it. Even if being honest about it was the only thing I ever did.

* * * * * *

If Lauren had only helped me figure out how to have feelings or helped me come to terms with being gay, she would have changed my life. But after my grocery store announcement, she realized that she was afraid I would find someone to be in a relationship with and we would lose our emotional intimacy. So, Lauren – who was kind, supportive, funny, beautiful and profoundly not gay – thought about her spectrum of sexuality and decided to relax a little. It just happened, completely by accident (or completely on purpose, depending on your view of the powers at work in the universe).

Unfortunately, I didn't feel like I could share my new relationship with my parents. I pulled away because I didn't want to lie to them. My sister would call sometimes and tell me how upset they were that I wasn't calling (remember, no one ever talks to anyone directly), but I didn't know what to do about it. I knew if I was honest with them, it would break their hearts. For two and a half long years, I did nothing. I called home irregularly. I sent them funny greeting cards on holidays. I went home for Christmas, mostly to celebrate my mother's birthday on Christmas Eve. Time passed. I felt worse and worse and worse.

I loved my parents, yet I was destroying the little bit of relationship I had with them. Our interactions were insubstantial, rooted in blood not in any real emotional connection. One day, I decided that I couldn't take it anymore. I had to tell them the truth, even if it meant they would never talk to me again. In my heart, I hoped that wouldn't be the outcome, but I knew it might. Because, even if I believed that God loved me, no matter what my orientation, that didn't mean my parents would or that they wouldn't be ashamed or embarrassed. On July 25, 1994, I wrote them a letter.

> Dear Mom and Dad,
>
> I am writing to tell you something that I have thought about telling you for some time. As you might have already guessed, I am involved in a relationship with Lauren. You don't know Lauren very well, but she is a wonderful, kind and generous soul. I am truly lucky to have her in my life. Our bond is a great source of joy and love and laughter for me and the relationship has brought a texture to my life it has never had before.
>
> I have probably hurt you by keeping this from you as long as I did. It was not out of any selfishness or malice on my part, but more out of sense of protectiveness. I wasn't sure that you could handle it, but, more importantly, I wasn't sure that I was strong enough to handle you not handling it. But as I have become stronger, I now see that I have no right to protect you. I can only be honest with you and hope that your love for me will not change.
>
> In the near term, I do not expect you to find your way to joy or even acceptance about my relationship and I do not expect you to tell your friends and family. I understand how prejudiced and judging this world is.
>
> While I know all our lives would be much easier if this relationship were more "traditional," that is not the hand life dealt me. I hope one day you will see, as I do, that the challenges in this relationship, while difficult, are minor compared to the tremendous love and compassion I find within it.
>
> I am afraid that you will blame Lauren for the difficulties we have had over the last couple of years. To do so is unfair. My relationship with Lauren aside, the last three years have been a period of great change for me. I have

learned a lot about myself and about my hopes and dreams and fears, and it has been difficult for me to share all of this with you. Not because I didn't want to, but because I understood it so little myself. While I hope that we will be able to go forward and strengthen our relationship, I cannot promise you that it will be like it was, because I am not who I was. My hope is that our relationship will be better and I am committed to trying to make it so.

You might be wondering why I decided to write you a letter instead of telling you in person. It is because I have a feeling that this may be difficult for you and I want to give you some time to think about it, get angry about it, laugh about it, do whatever you need to do in order to process this revelation. I do, however, look forward to talking to you about this whenever you feel you're ready.

I signed it "With love, Jan," put it in an envelope addressed to my mother, and mailed it. Then I waited.

There was a period of silence. It lasted several days. I called my sister. She told me my parents had received my letter. She had talked to them. They were upset, especially my father. After a couple of days, my mother called me. She said I was a coward for addressing the letter to her and then she told me she loved me. My father called several days later in the middle of the afternoon, when he knew I wouldn't be home. He left a message on my answering machine. He, too, told me he loved me, crying as he said it.

My mother tried really hard to come to terms with my revelation. She asked me all the time what she had done to make me gay. I told her nothing, because that's what I believed. In the spring of 1995, Jewell decided to come to California, so she could get to know Lauren better. The next year, she dragged my father out for the same purpose. During that second visit, Jewell acted as a cheerleader, keeping conversations going during meals, telling Lauren stories of my early successes, and asking Lauren about her family and childhood. It was incredibly awkward; everyone was trying so hard to find a way to make it work.

Then, one morning as I was sitting and eating breakfast with my parents, Lauren headed downstairs to work out in the gym. As she left, my father said, "Work out for me, too, will you?" Thirty minutes later when she came back in the apartment, my father chastised her. "I'm not even sweating," he said. "You must not have worked out very hard." I looked at my mother, who was smiling, and I suddenly realized how far we had come. My father, setting aside all his own fears and prejudices, had reached out to the person I loved with a really bad joke.

* * * * * *

"You're everything I always dreamed you would be." After all the pain and heartache I had caused, how could that possibly be true? I wanted to talk to Jewell, ask her if she meant it, but, instead, I just watched as the nurse started to push her away for surgery. As they disappeared, John, Julie and I stood in the hallway waving, like we were on a train platform watching as Jewell left on a trip to the big city.

Questions I wish I'd asked my Mother •*Which pair of baby shoes in the blue bathroom are mine?* •*Why are there three antique quilts under my mattress?* •*What made her paint the ceiling of my childhood bedroom orange?* •*Does she know where the afghan Granny Nash made for me is, the one with the roses?* •*What is her favorite color?* •*How come she used to like to sleep late when I was a kid, but she stopped sleeping late when they moved to South Carolina?* •*Did she intentionally hold on to her accent while we lived in Chicago?*

HIT BY A BUS

> Journal, November 16 -- Tomorrow, Jewell will have surgery. And the world will change again. Please God, let it change for the better.
>
> Journal, November 18 -- I'm not sure about the date. What I am sure about is that the second to last line of the previous entry is a gigantic understatement.

* * * * * *

We were all waiting in my mother's assigned hospital room when Dr. Puls, my mom's oncologist, came that afternoon and told us the surgery had been successful. All of the tumor sites had been "optimally debulked," meaning reduced to less than two centimeters, a good thing in ovarian cancer terms. But, five hours later, when Jewell hadn't returned from the recovery room, another doctor arrived. Jewell had sent her, the doctor said. "She knew you guys would be worried."

This doctor explained that my mother's blood pressure hadn't stabilized. Dr. Puls was on his way back to the hospital. As soon as he could, he would come up and give us a complete report. My aunt June, who is a nurse, and my cousin, Karen, who is a pharmacist, started asking questions. I only remember one, "Is she in DIC?" No, the doctor assured us, she wasn't. The doctor told us not to worry. Everything was going to be fine.

At about nine o'clock, Dr. Puls called up and talked to my father. My mother was going back into surgery. He would come and see us when it was over.

I started roaming the halls and eventually ended up at a window, just staring toward the dark hospital grounds below. Karen came over and put her arm around my shoulders. I asked her what was going on. She offered a couple of theories that I don't remember. And then I asked what "DIC" was and why she had asked about it. "It's an unpredictable and difficult to treat bleeding condition," she said. "People lose the ability to clot. They just bleed." "So," I asked stupidly, "it's bad." "Really bad. Which is why I wanted to make sure Jewell didn't have it."

Just at that moment, I turned and looked down the hall and saw Dr. Puls walking towards us with another man. Everyone came out of room 681 to meet them. "Mr. Nash," Dr. Puls said, "this is Dr. Miller. He's the head of the trauma unit here at the hospital. He was in the building and was kind enough to come in and assist me with your wife's surgery." Dr. Miller extended his hand toward my father. "Your wife is hemorrhaging. She has something called DIC bleeding..." Dr. Miller went on to explain what it was, but, I didn't listen, I already knew. Karen had told me ten seconds earlier. DIC bleeding was something you really didn't want to have.

Dr. Miller told us that every one of the "optimally debulked" sites was now leaking blood. He had packed Jewell's abdomen, trying to create pressure, and they were giving her drugs and blood, but now... there was nothing else they could do. We would have to wait and see what happened. "Do you have any questions?" Dr. Miller asked my dad. "I don't understand what you've said well enough to ask questions. All I heard was you saying that my wife is in trouble." "Yes, sir," the doctor responded, "she's in big trouble." Dr. Miller told us he would come back and get us when Jewell was transferred to the intensive care unit (ICU), so we could see her. He didn't say it, but I heard "just in case" as the subtext.

* * * * * *

My father could be described as a warm-hearted nerd. He's a quiet, generally good-natured man, with a dry sense of humor. He's affectionate and, for some reason, has a soft spot for cats. More than anything other than his family and friends, he loves computers. He can sit for hours and do... who knows what he's doing? Loading and unloading programs, trying new gadgets, surfing around the Internet looking for the best price on some piece of equipment he already owns. As long as he has time for his computers, he is perfectly willing to go along with whatever anyone else wants to do. While my mother was actively engaged in whatever was happening at the moment, my father would sit in the background quietly watching, listening.

He keeps his feelings to himself. Even a simple question like "How are you today?" elicits a benign or amusing response along the lines of "Pretty good, considering my age and aptitude," rather than a real answer. Information must be extracted from John; it will never be volunteered.

So, it was discomfiting when he went into the small bathroom of room 681 and, after a minute, Julie, Karen and I heard him crying and praying. "Please be with Jewell. Why did this have to happen?... What has Jewell ever done?... Don't take her away... I can't live without her..." Julie, Karen and I looked at each other. What were we supposed to do? I'd never dealt with my father when he was suffering. "Leave him alone," my sister mouthed to me. But I couldn't. I walked over to the door and knocked quietly. "Dad, are you okay? Can I help you?" He didn't answer.

After a minute, he came out of the bathroom and sat down next to us. No one said anything.

* * * * * *

Dr. Miller came and got us about an hour later. He led us through the back hallways and employee elevators to the ICU. He told us to go in a couple of people at a time. I walked in with my father and my sister. Jewell was lying on a bed toward the back of the room. Her whole body was swollen. There were small tubes sticking out of her nose, a ventilator tube sticking out of her mouth. A red dot glowed from some device attached to her finger. Her eyes were closed. Her skin was a weird, purplish-gray color. I stood there, looking at someone who vaguely resembled someone I loved. I was overwhelmed by a feeling of helplessness.

I had spent weeks focused on cancer. I had researched cancer. I had books about cancer. I had prayed about cancer. Cancer was the problem. I wasn't prepared for bleeding to death.

And yet, she was.

THE VISITOR

The doctors had done all they could. Jewell, with God's help, had to do the rest. All we could do was wait... and try to sleep so the time would go faster.

Room 681 was not designed to accommodate the sleeping needs of four, full-sized adults. My father lay down on the hospital bed. Julie took the "pull-out" chair/bed. Karen and I had to make do with the small armchairs. We tried every conceivable configuration: sitting in one chair with our feet on another; pulling two chairs together to make a small bed-like surface in the middle; lying down with our head and shoulders in one chair, feet and shins on the other, our midsection unsupported over the floor. We were really uncomfortable. Which wasn't a big deal: sleeping was impossible.

I kept looking over at my father. I knew he was thinking what I was thinking. How did this happen? Was she going to die? If she did, what would we do without her? All those questions, all that fear, were running through my mind as I lay in my two horrible little chairs waiting for morning.

At 3:20 a.m., the hair stood up on the back of my neck. Suddenly, I could barely breathe. I felt an energy move through the room. I knew what it was. It was Jewell. Her presence was all around me. I knew, in that moment, she was dead. She had come to make sure we were okay or to say "goodbye." Something. My eyes darted back and forth across the room, trying to see her.

I looked at my father, my sister, Karen, wondering if they could feel what I was feeling, but they lay still. No one seemed alarmed. So, I tried to calm my breathing and, after a moment, the sensation faded. I laid there, my heart pounding, wondering what was happening down in the ICU.

* * * * * *

Sometimes, I think it would be easier to believe in nothing. Instead, I have an active belief in God and his power to work in the world, as well as a strong belief in the continued life of a soul after death. Not just in a biblical "heaven is a place where angels fly and the streets are paved with gold" kind of way, but more like "grandmothers hang around after they're dead and take care of unfinished business."

Jewell's mom, Julia Collins, haunted her own home after she died: turning lights off and on and dropping things. She kept at it until my mother and her siblings worked out the arrangements for taking care of their disabled sister, Brenda. Once everything had been settled, Julia went away and never came back. After Lela Belle, my father's mother, passed away, her spirit came to me in church for about two years, usually when the congregation or the choir sang one of those old-fashioned church hymns.

My grandmother Nash had been a devout Southern Baptist and, when my sister and I visited her as children, she dragged us to the Nash Grove Baptist Church whenever they opened the church doors. Sunday mornings, Sunday evenings, Wednesday evenings. If a bunch of people were gathered in God's name, we were there. The congregation used to sing all of those great songs: "What a Friend You Have in Jesus," "How Great Thou Art," "Rock of Ages." Granny played the organ. My sister and I sat in the front pew, trying not to be bored.

Lela Belle and I had a strained relationship. I thought she was narrow and she thought I was out of control. We loved each other, but our relationship wasn't warm. Suddenly, for reasons I didn't understand, old religious songs were bringing her back to me. I don't mean emotionally. I mean, she came back. A song would start and I would become conscious of her energy hovering over my left shoulder, near my ear. I knew it was Lela

Belle. I don't know how I knew. I just knew. I could feel her. It was a warm, loving sensation and it made me feel really bad that I hadn't been nicer to her when she was alive. I almost always cried.

She visited me for two years. I never told anyone about it. Lela Belle and I kept this silent bond as I moved from city to city, church to church. Then, after I moved to Los Angeles, I casually mentioned to Lauren that my dead grandmother came to me. "Do you talk to her?" Lauren asked. "No," I replied. "She's dead." "Well, she's coming back for something. You might want to find out what it is."

The very next week, as I sat alone in a strange church, the organ began to play and Lela Belle magically appeared. I sat quietly for a moment, wondering what to do and then I said, "Granny?" Instantaneously, the words "Always remember" flashed into my mind and just as quickly, I realized Lela Belle was gone. The song kept playing, but the familiar energy I had come to associate with my grandmother had vanished. "Granny! Don't go." I pleaded. But I knew she had. I was left with a puzzle. "Always remember." What the hell did that mean?

I asked Lauren. She didn't know. So, I called my sister, Julie, and, somewhat reluctantly, told her the whole story of my two-year relationship with our dead grandmother. I expected mocking, after all that's what siblings do. But, when I finished my story, Julie simply said, "How come this happens to you? I was nice to Granny. Why didn't she come and see me?" I told her I didn't know. Did she have any idea what Lela Belle was trying to say? "You know," Julie said, "for a really smart person, sometimes you can be really stupid." She told me that Lela Belle was trying to say that all was forgiven. I should let go of my guilt about our relationship and always remember the love we shared not the little things that kept us apart.

Lela Belle never came back.

* * * * * *

That experience made it impossible for me to dismiss what had happened in the hospital room. I couldn't explain it, but I knew Jewell had moved among us. Something had happened. I just didn't know what. I waited. No doctors or nurses came to deliver bad news. The next day, Jewell was still alive. I told my sister what I had felt in the room the night before. This time, she couldn't explain it either.

The next afternoon, the doctors operated a third time to remove the packing materials they had put in Jewell's abdomen the night before. Several days later, they took the respirator tube out of her mouth, and let us talk to her. My father held her hand. My sister, Karen and I stood around the bed while my mother looked up at us, confused. "Where's Daddy?" She asked. We didn't answer. We just looked at each other. Finally, Karen said, "You mean John? He's right there." Karen pointed at my father. "Is Julia here?" My mother wanted to know. Karen's daughter is named Julia, so she told Jewell that Julia was at home in Columbia. But the minute my mom asked about Julia, I knew she was talking about her own parents, Julia and Paul Collins. She had seen her parents. Jewell may have only been dead for an instant, but they were there, standing in the white light waiting for her. And now, a couple of days later with the respirator tube out of her throat, she finally got to ask where they had gone.

    I never asked her about floating into room 681. I never asked her if she thought she had died. I never asked her why she had chosen to come back to us.

SCRIBBLES

Jewell spent a week in the ICU. It was a disconcerting, cacophonous place. Ten patients, all of them desperately ill, arrayed on the edges of a single, large room. Every one of them is hooked up to a machine that beeped constantly, like the steady rhythm of a heartbeat. If one of the bodily functions it monitors went out of whack, the machine began to shriek. Initially, this sound horrified me, but it elicited almost no response from the nurses. They would drift over, cast a casual eye toward my mother and punch a button on the faceplate of the instrument. The shrieking would stop. After a couple of days, I decided that if these capable professionals didn't care, I wouldn't care either. After awhile, I stopped hearing it altogether.

It was not the only piece of equipment tethered to my mother. She was on a respirator for two days. A catheter in her urethra collected urine, a nasal gastric tube running down her nose and into her stomach sucked out her digestive juices. She had an epidural for pain, a bag full of a blue liquid for food, and two tubes sticking into her lower belly collected the ascites fluid still being produced in her abdomen. Jewell was a mess. And all of this paraphernalia annoyed her. She particularly hated the ventilator tube, mostly because she couldn't talk to us. It was almost impossible for her to communicate what she wanted. We would stand over her bed, guessing: Water? Washcloth? You're cold? You're hot? You're in pain? Do you need a nurse? Want me to get a doctor? Want me to stop asking questions? Either she was too weak to laugh or it just wasn't funny.

******

When we weren't with her, we just hung around, waiting impatiently for the hours to pass until our next fifteen-minute visit. The four of us, John, Julie, Karen and I, stayed pretty close to Jewell, afraid something bad would happen in our absence. I cried all the time: alone, in groups, with relatives, with strangers. My sister lost her composure only once, that first night when we went to visit Jewell in the ICI after her second surgery. After that, Julie didn't cry. She just stood around, being brave or helpful, whichever was required.

******

I was born ten months to the day after my parents got married. My sister was born four and a half years later, while my father was serving with the army in Stuttgart, Germany. I hated my sister. Into the peaceful life I had as an only child came this screaming bundle of yuck, and for some reason I was supposed to be happy about it. I'm told that, soon after they brought Julie home, I asked to hold her and promptly dropped her on her head.

What I disliked so intensely about her was the double standard that applied to our upbringing. My parents were very strict with me. I lived in a world of "yes, sirs" and "no, ma'ams." I had chores. If my father told me to do something, I did it, because I knew what the consequences were if I didn't. My father says that I knew exactly how far I could go before I could get into trouble.

Apparently, my sister had no idea where that line was or no fear of crossing it. Either way, to my slightly older eyes, she lived a carefree life without any of the restrictions that I embraced so freely. She stayed up later than I had been allowed to. She watched more television. She talked back. She didn't put her dishes in the dishwasher. It made my blood boil. So, I took it upon myself to act as a "defacto" parent, the person who enforced the strict code that Julie was ignoring. I would tell her to pick up her clothes. She would say "no." I would tell her she had to. She would tell me to mind my own business. I would tell her I was going to tell Mom. And she would respond with some version of "you ain't the boss of me." Eventually, we were screaming and whacking each other.

Now, we didn't fight all of the time, just a lot. And we kept fighting until I went away to college. Somehow, separation caused all those years of resentment to melt away; as did the fact that she had gotten bigger than me and could inflict some real bodily harm.

We couldn't be more different. I am bookish and share my mother's love of luxury hotels. Julie builds things and goes on camping trips. I will hug anyone. Julie gives out hugs like they were gold bars, something that should be stored in a vault and removed only for very special occasions. I have drifted through much of my life, allowing many of my choices to be made for me. Julie, for the most part, has moved through hers with a clear sense of who she was and of what she wanted to do.

After she graduated from college, Julie became a police officer. She does the job really well. She has a strong sense of right and wrong, a self-less devotion to her department and her city. It makes sense to me that she loves that job. She protects people from lawlessness, from bullies. I think she's protecting the world from people like the twelve-year-old me.

* * * * * *

Jewell was still in the ICU but stable when Julie had to go back to work. It was hard for her, but my dad and I told her that Jewell was going to be okay. She should go. Before she left, Julie sat down in a chair and wrote my mother a note. Jewell wasn't completely lucid, so Julie made me promise that I would give it to her later and tell Jewell that Julie didn't want to leave. She had to leave. I promised Julie I would.

I never read the note, but I know Jewell kept it. I've seen it, lovingly folded with "Mom" scribbled on the top, lying in the bottom right hand drawer of my mother's dressing area.

COMING OF AGE

Jewell finally developed active bowel sounds (which meant her intestines were working and she was recovering from surgery) and they moved her to the "step-down" unit, which is a less intense version of intensive care. She got her own room and, finally, some peace and quiet. The lights and monitors of the other patients wouldn't keep her awake. The nurse to patient ratio was only one to five, instead of one to two, but Jewell seemed to be holding her own, so the peace and quiet seemed like a good trade-off.

The nurse told her she had to try and go to the bathroom. He sat her up on a portable toilet. Her weak body slumped forward. I went over and let her lean on me for support. She started to cry. "I don't think I can do this?" "Do what, Mom?" I asked, pretending that I didn't know. "Live through this. It hurts too much. I don't think I can stand it."

In the ICU, Jewell kept asking everyone what had happened to her. My father explained it. Aunt June explained it. Karen explained it. I explained it. But she never remembered what we said. Or she didn't want to remember.

As I stood there now, her tears wetting the front of my shirt, she pleaded again to know what had happened to cause her so much pain. I told her again. During her first surgery, she had developed a bleeding disorder. The doctors operated two more times: once to pack her so she'd clot, once to remove the packing materials. She'd been in the ICU for a week. Hopefully, she'd move to a regular room in a couple of days. I leaned down and looked in my mother's face. "Do you have any more questions?" She shook her head. "I still don't know what happened to me," she said. "No, you don't." I replied. I stood up, pulled her head against my chest and tried to cry gently, so I wouldn't disturb her as she went to the bathroom.

I thought about how strange this all was. Three weeks before, my life was normal. Two weeks before, my mom just had cancer. Now, she had almost died, but then… she didn't. I'd looked at my mother's stools, watched her vomit bile into a basin, and, now, was holding her in my arms as she cried, afraid that she wouldn't have the strength to go on living. The familiar rhythms of our lives had been blown to shit.

* * * * * *

My parents moved to South Carolina in 1990. Since then, my mother had transformed. In the twenty-three years we'd lived in Wheaton, Illinois, my mother had never thrown a real party. I don't even remember her ever having anyone over for dinner. My sister and I used to have an annual pool party (we didn't have a pool, so swimsuits were optional) and we had hosted a big party for Jewell and John's 25th anniversary, but, in all those years, Jewell only hosted one event of her own: a brunch, for a beloved next door neighbor who was moving to Florida. I think she just didn't feel comfortable.

She grew up in rural South Carolina, right near the border of Georgia and nowhere. She was the oldest of six children: five girls – Jewell, Wilma, Brenda, Anna Reed and Hilda – and one boy, Jack. The family was poor. Their unpainted wood frame house had no indoor plumbing and no running hot water; a wood-burning stove provided its only heat. They peed in chamber pots or walked up the hill to the outhouse. They grew their own vegetables and slaughtered their own hogs. My grandfather Paul kept bees. My grandmother Julia sewed the kid's clothes, which were handed down until they were worn out, and then she turned the clothes into quilts. It is a life that, because I haven't lived it, I can't really understand.

My mother always spoke fondly of her upbringing. One of her favorite comments was that "We had a lot of love, even if we didn't have much of anything else." But I think that childhood, for all its good, cast a long shadow over my mother's life. I don't think she ever felt like she was good enough, at least when we lived in Illinois. Maybe it was her accent, or her upbringing. Maybe it was that she didn't go to college. Maybe she was just insecure. Who knows? Whatever it was, Jewell didn't really come out of her shell until my parents moved back to South Carolina.

Suddenly, surrounded by family and friends who shared her heritage and her accent, she started doing things. She joined a church, and she and my father became regular members of the senior's Sunday school class. She participated in two local garden clubs. My parents played bridge once a month. Jewell started taking weekend trips with friends and family, heading off to the mountains or the beach with barely a moment's notice.

But even more telling, my mother began to throw parties. Not just occasionally, she threw them all the time. It seemed like I couldn't call the house without hearing some sort of social event going on in the background. She threw parties for birthdays and babies and retirements. She hosted my cousin Kathy's wedding in her backyard. She invited the whole family over for Christmas. She even had a regular party on the Fourth of July for the balloon festival in Greenville. When the balloons got rerouted and stopped flying over her house, my mother kept holding the event. Sausage and ham biscuits, Bloody Mary's and muffins, every Fourth of July, starting at 9:00 a.m. She always threw a fun party and the tablecloths, napkins and decorations were always appropriate to the occasion.

Jewell came of age at fifty-three. Now she was only sixty-one. She still had a lot of things to do.

ICU

The hospital had kicked us out of room 681 on the day after my mother's first two surgeries. We were forced to hang out and sleep in the ICU waiting room with all of the other people who had friends or relatives in the ICU. There were always more people than there were chairs. And the chairs, if you got one, were uncomfortable. There were televisions at two sides of the room, but it wasn't clear who had control of the remotes. We were always watching some bad talk show. New people would constantly stream into the waiting room, their panic in stark contrast to the tired resignation of the people who had been sitting in the ICU for three or four or, in our case, seven days.

For all its discomfort, the place had a certain warmth. People took care of each other. We staked out a cluster of chairs in one area and, even when we left the room, no one took them. The people sitting around us were clearly guarding our spots. I became very aware of these people and the medical crises they were facing. I introduced myself to some, but others were just known as the "family of the man who was in the auto accident" or the "wife of the man who didn't come out of the anesthesia" or the "sister of the elderly woman who died." We kept track of their patient's progress: rejoiced if someone moved out of the ICU to a regular room or mourned with those who loved ones died or suffered a setback. I said more prayers for people I didn't know that week than I have any time in my life. And I know that same group of strangers was praying for us, "the family of the woman with cancer who almost died in surgery."

> ***Questions I wish I'd asked my Mother*** •*When she was a nurse, what was the grossest thing she ever saw in a hospital?* •*Was she there when Granny Collins died?* •*What is her favorite movie? Favorite book? Favorite dessert?* •*When did she know I was gay?* •*What did she think was happening my first two years of college, when I drank a lot and seemed depressed all the time?* •*When she was a kid, what did she dream of?* • *When I was a kid, what did she think I would be when I grew up?* •*What did she think my sister would be?* •*Did she worry that Julie and I would never learn how to get along?* •*If she could change anything about herself, what would it be?*

WHAT FILLS THE SPACES

> Journal, November 24 -- Jewell moved back into her original room today. One week late. We settled her in and I was getting ready to go home. Dad went into the bathroom and I was talking to Mom. She patted the bed and asked me if I wanted to lie down next to her. She put her arm around me and we laid there, crowded into the tiny hospital bed. She was patting my shoulder. I was patting her arm. I thought to myself, "never forget this."

> Journal, March 9 -- I just reread the last several entries. I got to the last one, the part about "never forget this" and I realized I already had. Something that, in the moment, was so powerful and all consuming slipped from my consciousness.

There is a big time leap between those two entries. Nothing was cut from my journals. Nothing existed. And there's a good reason: nothing bad happened. Jewell left the hospital, went home and started chemotherapy, taking Taxol and Carboplatin every twenty-eighty days. Her hair fell out, she was faintly nauseous and incredibly tired, but slowly her

CA-125 level (the somewhat imprecise measure of the ovarian cancer antibodies in her blood) began to fall. It started at eighty-five. By March, after five treatments, it was at fifteen. She was responding. After all Jewell's suffering, it seemed like a miracle.

I don't really remember anything else that happened during this period, though I have a vague memory of the birthday toast we gave her on Christmas Eve. It was some version of "Yeah, you're balding. At least you're not dead." It seemed festive at the time.

Those four months are the opposite of the Challenger disaster. For some reason, only pain registers sharply in my memory. I mean, I only remember four events from my entire early childhood: three of them are traumatic. I vomited on a cruise ship when we moved to Germany. I was two. I jumped off a swing and landed on a hatpin, which pierced my foot. I was three. And my parents brought my sister home from the hospital after she was born (yes, this counts as traumatic). I was four. My one good memory is much less clear. It's something about puppies.

So, the four months after my mother didn't die when she was recovering from surgery and responding to chemotherapy is like puppies. I know it was good, but I don't remember anything more specific about it.

* * * * * *

Somewhere in the middle of nothing bad happening, I got the idea that I should start meditating. I don't know why. It just appeared in my consciousness. I had this feeling it would help me. So on April 6, 1998, I bought a zafu, a small, round cushion that a lot of people use during meditation. I brought it home, put it in my office and sat down. Now what?

I developed my own system. I would pray for awhile, maybe read the Bible. I'd sit with my eyes closed and breathe. It wasn't very scientific. I just tried to empty my mind, to calm down a little. I tried to release my fears, turn them over to God or the Universe or whatever higher power might be listening. It sounds stupid, but it worked. I was calmer. Some days, "My mother has cancer... my mother has cancer... my mother has cancer..." scrolled across my supposedly blank mind. "I suck at my job" was another popular theme, as was "I'm a bad person" and "I need to buy peanut butter." But, between the fears and the grocery list, there were days when I felt really good, like God put his hand on the top of my head so I would know he was there.

* * * * * *

My spiritual background is pretty vanilla. My parents were raised as Southern Baptists and our family stayed Baptists right up to the moment when we stopped going to church. For most of my childhood, we would go to church on Sundays and then go to brunch. Eventually, we dropped church. Brunch, however, was sacred.

When I was a sophomore in high school, one of my favorite teachers led a Fellowship of Christian Athletes group for a bunch of my friends. As first, I went because all of my friends were going, but after awhile, I realized I liked it. So, I decided to give church another try. In Wheaton, Illinois, there were at least a million churches to choose from. I picked the one closest to my house. And as I moved from college to New York to Chicago to graduate school to Chicago to Los Angeles, I continued this less-than-educated church choosing method: I went close to home. Over the years, I have been Presbyterian, Episcopalian, Lutheran, non-denominational and Catholic. One week when I was out of town on business, I attended a Greek Orthodox service conducted entirely in Greek. I didn't understand a word. I still liked it.

Church has been the one constant in my life as I've changed jobs, moved away from family and friends, and been blissfully happy or profoundly depressed. It has been a refuge, a place where I could go and be connected to something outside myself, where the giant concerns of my life were put into proper perspective. In church, I was challenged to be the best version of myself, as much like God as I could be. I don't think it is an accident that my grandmother visited me in church because it is often the only place in my life where I am truly quiet, truly at peace.

At each step along the way, the closest church has, by happy coincidence, been the church I needed at that moment. In college, when I lived in my head, not my heart, I got an intellectual church. In Chicago, when my life was in chaos, I got a formal church, filled with comforting rituals. And, when I moved to Los Angeles, as I was learning to be more whole, I got the goofiest church of all time, Brentwood Presbyterian (BPC).

I remember my first Sunday at BPC. After a nice ten-minute walk downhill (the next closest church was fifteen minutes uphill and across a very busy street), I sat down and experienced an incredibly strange hour of religion. They met in the gym (though they later moved into their newly renovated sanctuary). The music sounded like it could have been sung around a campfire. The service included long periods when everyone would sit in silence. The congregation broke into applause with almost no provocation and, to make it even worse, they kept hugging each other. I referred to it afterwards as the "Zoom" church, because it felt like that PBS kid's show from the 1970's. But, I kept going. It was, after all, the closest church to my house and I wasn't going to abandon my decision-making criterion casually.

After a few weeks, BPC started wearing me down. They had this thing called "Celebrations of the People," where folks would go to the front of the sanctuary and talk about something good or bad that had happened to them. These stories were often heart breaking and, when these poor souls returned to their pews, I would watch as parishioners moved over and enveloped them in hugs or whispered words of comfort during the service. I saw people giving money to strangers who needed it and cheerfully scooting over to make room for a smelly homeless guy. These folks were actually listening to the minister's sermons and putting God's love into action.

Then one Sunday morning as I exited the sanctuary, the pastor, Charles Shields, hugged me without asking. As I skipped away humming the church's closing song, I realized I didn't need to walk uphill to another church. I liked BPC just fine.

* * * * * *

After my mother was diagnosed with cancer, I put a prayer request card in the offering plate at church. Several days later, a woman from the prayer chain called me at home. She wanted to send a note to my mother, to let her know that they were praying for her. I gave her my mother's address and thanked her. "Oh, dear. I'm happy to do it." She said. "Just as I'm happy to pray for you, too." And, then, with a loving "God bless you," she said goodbye.

> ***Questions I wish I'd asked my Mother*** •*Why did she decide to be a nurse?* •*What was it that made her love my father?* •*How was their first date?* •*When did he first kiss her?* •*How do I keep houseplants from dying?* •*What goes into the flour for fried chicken?* •*What is a basting stitch?* •*What did she and Granny Collins talk about when my mother was a girl?* •*Did she used to fight with her siblings?* •*Why did my parents wait so long to have my sister?* •*Why did she have a hysterectomy when I was in high school?* •*Did she know that she spent a lot of money and got anxious when the bills came?* •*How do I match patterns for upholstery?* •*How often do I need to weed a flowerbed?* •*Why did we stop going to church when I was in high school?*

ONE STEP FORWARD…

After Jewell had finished her first round of chemo, her CA-125 level was well below the target of thirty-five. The doctors told her she could have three more treatments, at her option. She asked if she could wait a couple of months and then decide. They said yes. So, she decided to wait. After all of the trauma of her surgery and the debilitating fatigue of chemotherapy, my mother decided she deserved a rest. She could finish those treatments later. For now, she wanted to feel good for a couple of months.

Jewell sent out postcards to her friends and family to celebrate her good response to chemotherapy. It was a photograph of her in all her hairless, shiny-headed glory. She's sitting draped across an armchair, a big smile on her face. On the back she had printed:

Dear Friends,

Happiness is: Hair; A normal CT scan; Cancer test CA-125 under 35 (mine is hovering around 15); Friends that love you, pray for you and keep you going when you don't feel like going...

Come to think of it, three out of four is not bad. The family and I thank you and send out love.

The postcard Jewell sent me is postmarked June 15. We didn't get to bask in the good news for very long.

<u>Journal, July 28</u> -- Mom calls from the car on the way out of the appointment. It's "bad news." The cancer is back. Her CA125 level is 35.

She is starting chemo this afternoon at one. Two new drugs with funny names that the doctors have had good success with. They think the chemo will start clearing up the fluid in 2-4 treatments. They don't want to drain her unless her breathing is affected.

She seems very upset. She can't believe she has to go through this. After I hang up, I realize that, while I've spent the last five days hoping for the best but preparing for the worst, she has spent that same time hoping this is a mistake. I've had five days to get used to it. For her, today, it is a new wound.

TWO STEPS BACK

Jewell's cancer began to produce a seemingly endless stream of medical procedures. We'd already been through the surgery and all of its complications and follow-up. Then there was the first round of chemo, once every twenty-eight days. Now we were into a second round of chemo, five days in a row every fourth week and that would be followed by the third round of chemo, which was really just the first round of chemo again because the second round of chemo didn't work. In the middle of all that poison, there was lab work (every Monday at the hospital's drive through blood lab), shots to deal with the impact of the chemo drugs and blood products to deal with the shots. At one point, she had outpatient surgery to install a port near her left collarbone. It was supposed to help with the second round of chemotherapy. The drugs could be injected directly into her system through the port, so the veins in her arms wouldn't suffer from overuse; the port never worked. She kept getting IVs. Over time, more and more of her veins shriveled and collapsed.

And, of course, there were pills. Lots and lots of pills. Jewell kept them all in a lunch box-sized Tupperware container. Every morning and every evening, she sat down at the kitchen table and methodically dispensed a pile of multicolored tablets. Compazine for nausea. Phenergan for nausea. Reglan for nausea. Ativan for anxiety. Pepcid to ease the burning in her stomach. She took some hormone to stimulate her appetite and, at various other times, different tablets and capsules were prescribed to solve the "problem du jour." On some days, Jewell ate more pills than food.

* * * * * *

I talked to my mother every day. And phone call after phone call, Jewell would reveal that day's piece of bad news. She didn't complain; she just rolled with the seemingly endless series of punches. It would have been funny if it hadn't been so darn sad.

> Journal, August 24 -- Jewell went to the doctor. Her port didn't work, so they gave her the chemo intravenously. She had to drink some dye for an X-ray to determine why the port didn't work. And they drained her... She said she felt more comfortable, though her mouth tasted like metal from the dye.
>
> "Like sucking on pennies?"

"Yes, just like that. If I'd ever had a reason to suck on pennies."

<u>Journal, September 2</u> -- I called home early this morning (about 9:00 my time) and Mom answered.

"Hello?"
"Hey, it's me."
"Can I call you back? I'm on my way out to the doctor's."
"Okay. Is anything wrong?" I remembered that she had blood work tomorrow.
"Oh, I have a little shortness of breath and my ankles are swollen. They are going to do a chest x-ray. So, I'll call you later."

I said goodbye and hung up. And then I realized, I had no idea what these symptoms might mean. Lauren tried to keep me calm. "We don't know anything." And, while I parroted that bit of wisdom back to her, I got in the car and cried all the way to work. I have this morbid tendency whenever I'm faced with what might be bad news to start planning my outfit for the funeral.

They didn't call by noon, so I called and left a message. They didn't call by 3:00, so I called again. My dad answered the phone and he sounded chipper, so I assumed that the news wasn't horrible. My mom got on the phone (my dad informed me she was buck naked) and sounded good.

"What were the swollen ankles all about?"
"Oh, apparently the fluid build-up compresses my heart and lungs, so they don't work as well and then my circulation isn't as good and the fluid builds up in low places. They think I might have a little congestive heart failure. If the fluid doesn't clear up by Friday, they're going to give me a diuretic to deal with it. They didn't want to do anything else to me today."

"I guess you can have too many medical procedures in one day."
"Oh, definitely."

She sounded good. So, the words "congestive heart failure" never really sank in. She didn't seem worried, so I didn't get worried. But after I hung up, it occurred to me that it was probably not a good thing. My sister had the good sense to think of this during her conversation with my mother.

"Congestive heart failure... isn't that a big deal?"
"Not if you have cancer."

Journal, October 22, 1998 -- I called today and asked how she was.

"Oh, I'm having a 'great day.'"
"I can't tell. Are you being serious or sarcastic."
"I have pneumonia."

My Aunt June told her that if she didn't have bad luck, she'd have no luck at all.

Jewell went to the doctor because she had a pain in her port. The doctor examined her and said he thought she had pneumonia. He sent her for a chest x-ray. Jewell said she didn't believe it; she didn't feel that bad. But the chest x-ray came back positive. They were going to prescribe a new antibiotic... The last thing I said to my mother was "I'll add pneumonia to the long list of things I'm already praying about."

Journal, October 24 -- So, last night, I'm standing on stage, enjoying the "sleep together" episode of "Caroline in the City" and Heather, Neil and Gary's assistant, walks over and says, "Jan?"

I turn toward her and, in a very deliberate and sympathetic way, she says, "Your dad called. Your mom's in the hospital." She hands me a message slip. "He says it's not an emergency, in fact he told me I didn't need to get you. But I thought you'd want to know." I just stared at the message slip.

I continued to stare at the message for what felt like ten minutes and was probably ten seconds. [Then] I lifted up the yellow caution tape, whispered "Thank you" to Heather and started walking toward my office. In the elevator, Heather continued to relay the story of how she volunteered to come get me and how my dad didn't want her to.

I called Jewell's [hospital] room and dad picked up. Jewell had a blood clot.

Apparently, he had told her to tell the doctor about the discomfort in her neck and she had forgotten to do it. So, in the afternoon, John paged the doctor and told him that she was stiff on the left side of her neck and a little puffy. The doctor told him to take her to the hospital to have it looked at. After some sort of "Doppler" test, they admitted her. She has to stay for six days while they move her from [intravenous] heparin to Coumadin and break down the clot. She is having her port (the source of the clot) removed on Monday...

I talked to her a couple of times today. She sounds weak, but okay. Lauren, who also talked to her, said my mom was relieved to at least know why she was feeling the way she was feeling.

The whole thing has thrown me. I've been praying for a week that Jewell's CA-125 test would be down. I didn't know I was also supposed to be praying that she wouldn't get pneumonia or a blood clot. Lauren suggested we just get a medical book and start praying for the "a's" and work our way back. Julie volunteered to start with the "z's" and work her way forward.

I am unable to deal with the number of different medical crises. The ones we've already been through don't even warrant consideration anymore. I get so focused on a specific thing – wishing Jewell felt better, for instance – that I don't even know how to react when she has a blood clot. Why does she need to have a blood clot? Isn't cancer enough?

I don't even think about the toll all of these other conditions must be having on her recovery.

I said to someone at the show last night, "You hate to have cancer then die of a blood clot." And then I repeated it to Julie this morning. Julie said, "You've jinxed her, Jan. Mom's not going to die of cancer. She's going to get hit by a bus. And none of us are going to see it coming."

Journal, October 28 -- Jewell seems to be doing fine. They removed the port on Monday. And they moved her off the heparin today and onto the Coumadin. She's had a lot of guests, all of whom have brought gifts. One woman made my mom a nightgown.

I think we would all be better people if we knew how and took the time to make people homemade nightgowns.

And through all this, Jewell kept producing ascites fluid. She would swell up and begin to look like she had a basketball strapped to her abdomen. The weight of it made her uncomfortable and tired. At a certain point, she would feel so "full" that she would have to go to the doctor's to get drained: four liters on July 31, seven liters on August 24, a gallon on September 2, a couple of quarts on September 14, eight liters on November

4, seven liters on December 14… almost eight gallons in all and these are just the appointments I happened to have written about in my journal. In between these "official" drainings, she often leaked. The holes created by the needles inserted into her abdomen wouldn't close and fluid would leak out of them, especially after the doctors put her on blood thinning medication for the clot. Sometimes Jewell covered the holes with a washcloth, sometimes with one or more Kotex pads. If it was bad enough, they would put a colostomy bag over the hole and let the fluid drip into it. Drip after drip, until the one-pint bag was full and had to be changed.

The ascites absorbed the nutrients from the food she was putting into her body. In effect, despite her efforts to eat as much as she could, she was malnourished. Her limbs began to swell up like sausages. My mother was puffy all over, like the Pillsbury doughboy.

* * * * * *

In the middle of all this medical upset, though I don't remember which particular event it was, Jewell was telling me about some drug the doctors had put her on and she stopped herself. "I don't need to tell you about this. I bet you know more about it than I do." She knew that, at every step up to this point, my compulsive need for control had driven me to research her treatments and pester her with questions to ask the doctors. "Did you find anything interesting on the Internet?" She asked. I told her not really and got off the phone quickly. I was stunned. I realized I hadn't done any research on this drug at all. When this new crisis cropped up, I had just absorbed it and moved on.

Questions I wish I'd asked my Mother •*Did she worry about me when I was traveling alone in Europe?* •*Did she come with me for two weeks to make sure that I was going to be okay?* •*Can she make Julie give me back the $18 in half dollars she stole from my piggybank?* •*When she was little, did she fight with her sisters?* •*If so, what did they fight about?* •*Did she have a good relationship with her father?* •*What did she used to do when she was a kid?* •*Did she like school?* •*Who was her first boyfriend?*

THE REST OF LIFE

Life did go on. For me, it was the most remarkable thing about my mother's cancer. Even though Jewell's cancer was the most important event going on in my life, groceries still needed to be bought, bills still needed to be paid, birthday cards still needed to be mailed and, strangest of all, people still expected me to show up for work.

* * * * * *

I worked as a writer on a television show. It was a fun job, kind of a cross between being an artist and a kindergartner. I felt very lucky to have it, maybe because I had so many less satisfying jobs before I got to it.

Looking back on my career path with the wisdom of hindsight, it kind of makes sense, like I knew what I was doing. But, I didn't. While I was the middle of it, I flailed around, wondering where the hell I was going in my life. Now, I can see the path hewn out of my indecision by God's clear hand. At almost every moment when a change needed to be made, an easy choice presented itself. And, being a person who likes easy choices, I always picked them.

I majored in American Studies at Stanford. It was an interdisciplinary major involving the study of history, English and political science. My choice wasn't driven by any particular intellectual fervor. I simply looked at my transcript one day and realized that I had taken almost half the courses to finish the major. It was easy, so, suddenly, I was an American Studies major. When I told my father what I had selected, he said "And it will prepare you to do what... vote?"

In the middle of my senior year, I looked around and realized I had no idea what to do with the rest of my life. My friend, Kathleen, had conducted a very focused and rigorous job search the year before, eventually landing a job as an analyst at First Boston, an investment bank. She set up an informational interview for me at her firm and, so, I flew to New York. I met with a nice man who seemed to like me. He had me meet with a few other people. By the end of the day, I had talked to about eight investment bankers and, as I was leaving, one of them told me he would call me. He actually did, and offered me a job. My whole job acceptance thought process went like this: "If I take this offer, I don't have to go on any more interviews; I can spend the whole spring quarter lying in the sun." I accepted the offer immediately.

The job search was easy. The job was not. I worked as an analyst in First Boston's mergers and acquisitions department, starting in New York and eventually moving to Chicago. I worked everyday, weekends included, often until the wee hours of the morning. I sat in front of a computer (thank God for the invention of computers, otherwise I would have been sitting in front of an abacus or something) and churned out page after page of financial analysis. I really liked the people I worked for and I was still eager to please, so despite my general loathing (and fear) of the work itself, I put in long hours and tried to do a good job. Kathleen calls this the "dark First Boston period," because I basically dropped off the face of the earth. No one ever heard from me and, if they did, I suspect I wasn't that fun to talk to.

I left First Boston, went to the Stanford Business School because I couldn't think of anything else to do and then went back to First Boston. Most people would have been able to avoid going back to a job they didn't really like, but I'm not most people. It was easy and I thought "easy" was good. I mean, I loved my boss. He was kind and decent and good at his job. And, he thought I was good at mine, so my own feelings about it didn't really matter. But, after awhile, the work began to feel so devoid of meaning that even I couldn't ignore the feeling.

At that very moment, God sent another job to me. I don't mean I looked for another job and got one. I mean I was sitting at my desk, pushing a button to run the one thousandth iteration of some merger proposal and someone called me to ask if I'd be interested in interviewing at Disney. Now, some people would view this as lucky. I don't believe in luck. I believe God, sure that I wouldn't be able to change my life on my own, delivered an opportunity to me I couldn't ignore. I mean, I'd always wanted to work in entertainment. Here was my chance. I was sure that this was going to be "it," the job that would give purpose to my life.

Well, as I've already mentioned, the job at strategic planning wasn't exactly what I'd hoped. My father used to describe his airline pilot job as "99% boredom, 1% sheer terror." My new Disney job was about 50/50. It was the worst job I've ever had. Horrible. Miserable. A "go-to-sleep-crying-wake-up-with-a-pit-in-the-bottom-of-your-stomach" kind of job. Really, really bad.

Viewed through the filter of hindsight, it's another God-given tiny step in my career path. I needed to be in Los Angeles so I could become a writer. And I couldn't become a writer unless I left strategic planning. The only way I was going to leave a secure, high paying job was if it was so miserable that I just couldn't stay. It was that miserable, so, I left. For the first time in my life, I was unemployed.

After two months of not figuring out what to do next, one of the nice people I'd worked with in strategic planning arranged for me to have an interview with the head of Disney's network television department. This man gave me a couple of scripts to read, listened pleasantly to my thoughts on them and then told me he didn't have any openings. I went home. A couple of weeks later, that same nice person from strategic planning called again and asked me if I'd followed up on my interview. I hadn't. He said I should. So, I did and found out that a job had opened up. They asked if I was interested.

I was. For the next three and a half years, I read scripts, watched television shows be filmed, met celebrities and generally ignored the feeling in the bottom of my stomach that this job wasn't quite right either.

My mother, when I first informed her I was thinking of leaving strategic planning, told me not to do it. She'd been a nurse her whole life; my father had been with the army for almost twenty years and with United Airlines for twenty-three. "I don't want people to think you're the kind of person who can't stick with things," Jewell told me. I'd ignored her advice then, but now I was starting to think she might be right. Maybe I was just chronically unsatisfied; maybe I couldn't stick with things. That fear would probably have kept me working as a television executive for a long time, except I realized that my mom had liked being a nurse and my dad had liked being a pilot. I should keep going until I found something I really liked.

So, I arranged a breakfast with my boss and, as we sat drinking coffee, I quit my job. I didn't mean to. My brain was screaming, "Stop it, you idiot," as my mouth kept moving and saying things like "I need to move on" and "I want to do something more creative." My boss, God bless him, looked at me and said, "Have you thought about what?" I hadn't. I panicked. I came to this breakfast to lay the groundwork for a change. Suddenly, I was making changes I hadn't planned. Fear compelled me to silence but for some reason I calmly said, "I'd like to work on a show. I want to be a writer." He told me he would support whatever I wanted to do. Less than a month later, I had my first job on a television show.

Now, in the interests of full disclosure, I feel I should share an experience I had many years before which would seem to make this whole long journey unnecessary. Once, way back in college, before I'd even decided to major in American Studies, I was flying back to school and pondering my future. What was I going to do with my life, I wondered? As I looked out the window at the blue skies and the carpet of white clouds below it, I heard a voice say, "Be a writer." This seemed like a good idea, so, of course, I did the only logical thing: I spent five years working at an investment bank; two years in business school; two years in corporate strategy; and four years in a television development job. Then I became a writer.

I like writing. I can imagine doing it for the rest of my life. I know Jewell will be relieved to hear that.

* * * * * *

I was working on "Hiller and Diller" during my mother's surgery debacle. I moved to "Caroline in the City" in June of the following year, a little bit before she relapsed. The executive producer of the show was very kind and supportive. He told me that I should visit Jewell whenever I needed to and talk to her as many times during the day as I wanted to and leave the room and lay down if I felt too sad to work. I took him up on all of these offers. I took two days off from work about every five or six weeks in order to fly to Greenville and see my parents. I talked to my mother from the office almost every day. It was hard. I would often hear about some medical setback or her emotional low and then I'd go back into the room and try to be funny.

I wish I'd been able not to care about my job. But I couldn't. "Caroline" was only the third show I had worked on and I was still proving myself. And, heck, I'm as insecure as the next person. I spent a lot of time worrying about what people thought of me. Was I contributing enough to the show? Were my jokes funny? When I opened my mouth to pitch something, did every other writer in the room silently pray, "Please God, let this not be too horrible"? From an ego perspective, it all mattered to me. On the other hand....

> Journal, December 2 -- Work has been very frustrating. I work hard. I pull my weight and then some. I'm always alert. I contribute. And yet, I always end up feeling bad.
>
> On the flip side, who gives a shit? It's a TV show and my mother has cancer.

* * * * * *

Despite her initial resistance to my job switching, Jewell loved that I worked in television because it meant I got to meet celebrities. She loved celebrities. She always wanted to talk about whether they were nice people and what kind of clothes they wore to work. On her trips to Los Angeles to visit me, she even got to meet a few, something she seemed to enjoy much more than any of the other activities I planned for her.

Jewell had already relapsed when I wrote my first "Caroline in the City" script. It included a bit where a couple dances in the background, behind one of our regular actors. In my script, as they come out to begin their dance, I had an announcer say, "Let's give a warm hand for John Nash... and his wife Jewell, the Tri-County Tango champions." Through the entire week of production, the only thing I cared about was getting my mother's name on television. Jokes I had struggled with came and went.

My laboriously crafted dialog got replaced. Entire scenes were thrown out. I didn't care. I just wanted Jewell to hear her name on television. My sister, Julie, told me later that when she talked to Mom the day after the episode aired, hearing her name was all she wanted to talk about.

> ***Questions I wish I'd asked my Mother*** •*Did she know that when Julie was little she treated her more leniently than she treated me?* •*What is parboiling and when do I do it?* •*Why didn't we travel as a family when we were young?* •*What were some funny things I did as a kid?* •*What were some funny things my sister did as a kid?* •*If she had all the money in the world, what would she buy?* •*Does she have any regrets?* •*What exactly is fatback?* •*What did she mean when she told me I was "destined for greatness" in high school?* •*Was she disappointed when I stopped playing competitive tennis at age sixteen?*

THERAPY

My mother always said she thought "therapy was a good thing," but apparently it was a "good thing" for other people, because she never tried it until she got cancer. Then, overwhelmed by the same uncertainties that were overwhelming all of us, she sought out the help of Dr. Miller. She liked him so much that she wanted all of us to talk to him.

We went as a family. She told each of us that the therapy was for the benefit of the other family members. When we got there, it became clear that the therapy was for me. I was overwhelming Jewell with my suggestions for alternative treatments: meditation, acupuncture, visualization, etc. She didn't think I was facing the reality of her situation. I assured her I was and, after that, I stopped pushing.

On another occasion, she told my sister and me that she was worried about my father; she thought he was keeping everything inside. She wanted Julie and I to go with him to therapy, hoping that, without her there, he would open up and share his fears. When the day of the appointment arrived, my dad went to get Jewell and she "reminded" him that she wasn't going. Of course, he had no idea. She never told him. Julie and I mocked her later for not being honest with him, but she stuck to her story. She was sure she had mentioned it. John was a little pissed off, but he went to Dr. Miller's anyway.

> Journal, August 28 -- We started the day in therapy – at least Dad, Julie and I did... Dr. Miller only made two points. The first was that if Jewell believes we think she can get better, she will feel like she let us down if she doesn't get better. The second was that we go through the process of grieving at lots of different points in life, not just when someone dies.
>
> After therapy, we came home and then... we went to the mall and mom bought some new glasses... Then we drove to Parisian. She bought several dresses. Big people's dresses. She wore one tonight to dinner. She looked beautiful. Her cute hair. New glasses. New dress. A little white over shirt. Funky triangular silver earrings. Suede shoes. Expensive Swiss watch. She looked normal. Except for the basketball sized sack she's carrying in her abdomen.
>
> I watch and I listen. Does she look uncomfortable. Is that burping gas? How much did she eat and what? Was that a yawn? I look for signs. How long? Will she suffer? Does she seem to be okay?
>
> And all she does is worry about us. Was dad okay in therapy? I told her he was and she should talk to him. He can handle it. I told her Julie was also okay. She should talk to Julie.

> The other thing I learned in therapy is that my mom
> is still pissing my dad off with her wild spending
> habits. Apparently, she wants to spend thousands of
> dollars on home and other projects. My dad doesn't
> want to do them, but he feels guilty denying her these
> small pleasures if she is going to die soon. Dr. Miller
> told him he could cut her some slack if he wanted,
> but he could also confront her. "Be straight with
> her," he said. "Jewell, if you die, I'm going to need
> money to live. And if you don't die, we're going to
> need money to live." It's amazing that, 38 years
> later, they still haven't worked out this issue.

* * * * * *

My pastor, Charles Shields, was diagnosed with prostate cancer several years ago. A letter arrived in the mail informing the congregation of his illness and that he would be taking some time off to focus his energies on healing. From what I could tell from my pew in the back right corner of the church, Charles began an intensive program of meditation, changed his diet (I think he went macrobiotic), and also followed his doctor's advice for a traditional medical approach to the cancer. His initial prognosis was bleak: four months. Charles survived those four months and then some, eventually returning to Brentwood Presbyterian Church full-time because the doctors had determined that he was in remission. In between that diagnosis and his remission, there were several ups and downs that must have struck fear into his heart and the hearts of his family and friends. It certainly struck fear into my heart, and I'm just someone who sits in the back of the church, listens to his sermons and thinks really well of him from a distance.

One Sunday, Charles preached a sermon on the crises that come into our lives and used his own cancer as an example of how these crises can bring us closer to God. He talked about being in remission and the things he had learned during his four-year dance with cancer. (Charles always calls his journey with cancer a "dance.") Then he said something I will never forget. He said he felt like he had "reached an agreement with cancer that they would peacefully coexist."

It reminded me of something that Dr. Miller had said to us during one of our family therapy sessions. He pointed out that the language our culture used to discuss illness is similar to the language we use for battle. It's about winning and losing. People say someone put up a "good fight" or they "gave it all they had." People have a "fighting chance" or "in the end the cancer was just too strong." Cancer is an "other," something we fear, an enemy that, like all good enemies, needs to be crushed. It is something within us that we hate, which takes an enormous amount of energy, both mental and physical, to destroy. "Maybe it would be easier," Dr. Miller said, "if we could just accept that cancer is part of life. Something to teach us the lessons we need to get to the next level."

WHAT WE WISH FOR

Journal, September 30 -- Today, I called and… She had
been to the doctor's office and seen Dr. Puls. He wanted
to put her back on Taxol and Carboplatin, because the
new drug didn't seem to be working. I asked her how she
felt.

"I feel good about my decision."

I asked again and I got the same answer. Julie said that
when she talked to her, she sensed that Jewell was upset.
She'd been let down, by her body or the drug or the
doctors. Something hadn't worked.

I think I live in fear that she will reach a tipping point.
There will be one piece of bad news that will push her
over the edge, cause her to lose hope. I'm always on
edge, wondering which piece of news it will be.

* * * * * *

My Aunt Wilma's husband, Howard, was diagnosed with inoperable pancreatic cancer about a month before my mother was diagnosed with ovarian cancer. The doctors had opened him up to remove the tumor and, when they saw it, just sewed him back up without even trying. They told his family that he had six months to a year. For a year, we watched him die. Little complications cropped up -- an intestinal obstruction, pressure sores on his hips, hallucinations from too much morphine. And then, finally, he died, a 130-pound shell of his former 220 pound self. His cancer, just like my mother's cancer, moved down its own path. It was like a river. The doctors might be able to divert it, but the water would keep flowing, relentlessly moving forward.

Uncle Howard was always in the back of my mind as I tried to figure out how to respond to the changes in Jewell's condition. What did Jewell need from me? What could I do to help her? Every fiber of my body told me, "Smile, tell her it's going to be okay," because hope feels like the one thing a sick person should have. And hope is really important. But, really, how do we know what we're supposed to be hoping for? How do we know we're all hoping for the same thing? And, if we're not, whose hope is the most important?

* * * * * *

At the beginning, I hoped for a cure. I wanted my mother to beat cancer and go on to live a long and happy life. I expected her to keep annoying me well into my sixties. We could have another thirty years together. After the relapse, with all the information I had at my disposal, a cure seemed unlikely. Was it too much to hope that she would be one of the lucky ones, surviving for longer than the eighteen-month statistical average? My mom was a fighter. She had good doctors. Why shouldn't she live for another three or four years? She just couldn't apparently. She was fighting, but she never got any traction in her recovery. So then, I stepped back and began to hope for some something less: a year maybe of good health, where she would be with us and do the things that she enjoyed.

> Journal, November 10 -- I called Mom this morning. She sounded a little ragged, but she told me she felt okay. I called tonight, and Dad tells me she's been vomiting all day, hasn't eaten and is running a slight temperature. He gave her a suppository. If she isn't better by the morning, she's going into the doctor's office for fluids.
>
> I don't know if she was lying to me [this morning], or if it was an honest answer. Maybe she was telling the truth; it's just that her version of "feeling okay" is skewed. Skewed to include vomiting.

Ours was a subtle journey of diminished expectations.

Journal, November 29 -- Jewell said she wasn't feeling well today. I asked her what was wrong.

"I'm just tired. I don't know why."
"I don't know, maybe it's cancer."
"That's probably it."

RUN

My sister had gone to visit my parents on one of her regular visits. I knew Julie would give me an honest assessment of my mother's condition. So, on Sunday morning, after Lauren left to go to yoga and before I left for church, I called my parents' house to ask how Jewell was.

> <u>Journal, November 15</u> -- Julie told me they had been to Karen's the night before for the chili party. Right then, she [was] laying on the bed with my mom watching television.
>
> "Does Mom look bad?"
> Silence.
> "Does Mom look bad, just answer 'yes' or 'no'"
> Silence
> "Are you there?"
> "Yes."
> "Are you worried?
> "No… I had two kinds of chili."
> "Nice transition. Will you call me back?"
> "Sure."

She called me back. She said that for the first time, Mom looked worse than she expected her to. She thought that I should come home... Mom looked thin and she's always tired.

"But I'm not giving up hope.'
"Of course you're not. You're just being realistic."

She told me to call Aunt June, who would give me the straight scoop.

"Don't ask Dad. He'll just say 'no' because he wants to believe everything's going to be okay."

* * * * * *

I called my Aunt June to ask if she thought I should come home. She said she didn't know. I think her exact words were, "I don't want to be alarmist, but you never can tell about these things." She finally said it certainly wouldn't hurt anything and it might just make my mother feel a little better. I hung up. I realized I was late for church. I ran out of the house and got to church after it had started. I sat in my normal pew. After about fifteen minutes of discreetly drying my eyes and trying to control my emotions, I left. I wasn't comfortable crying in front of strangers.

> Journal, November 15 -- When I got in my car to leave church, I laid my head against the steering wheel and sobbed. I know my mother is going to die. And I know there is nothing I can do about it. As much as I want it to be different, it's not going to be. She is going to slowly fade away from us. One little bit at a time. And the woman I knew, the one I loved, is already gone. I should

have the grace to say "goodbye" to the shell that is left, but I don't.

* * * * * *

Lauren and I have a small white box with angels on top of it. We call it our "God Box." Anne Lamott, a favorite author, had written about her own "God Box" at some point, and it seemed like a good way of dealing with the stresses of our everyday lives. We'd write whatever problem was bothering us on a slip of paper or post-it or the edge of a magazine subscription card. We'd fold it up, put it in the box, and say a prayer about the problem. The prayers were usually of the form "God, we're having a lot of trouble dealing with "X." So, we've put it in our 'God Box.' We give it to you. Thanks for your help."

The box sits on a ledge in the bedroom. We don't think about it much, unless we have a problem to put into it. Occasionally, we clean it out, pull out the remains of yesterday's problems and weed through the ones that no longer apply. It's usually amusing. Almost always, the issue has resolved itself. What seemed insurmountable is over. The same types of problems appear over and over and over again, as if our whole lives were being filtered through the lens of work or self-esteem or (insert your problem here). Sometimes, the message on the paper is short-handed and we can't even figure out what problem it was meant to address. These lapses help put things in perspective. If something was all-consuming one minute and forgotten only a short while later, maybe whatever I'm facing today isn't that big of a deal.

We had mentioned the "God Box" to Jewell and she liked the idea of putting her problems into it and turning them over to God. So we decided to give her one for Christmas. We had bought a simple wooden box at Pottery Barn which had a space in the middle of its lid for a small photograph. We hadn't decided what picture to put in it. Sitting on my zafu in my dark office that morning, all I could think of was that I had to give my mother her "God Box" right away. Maybe it would help her. So, I dug through our photographs and found one. It was a picture I'd taken a couple of years earlier at Yellowstone. A geyser erupting against a dark sky with a small burst of sunlight illuminating the geyser itself, as if God were bursting from the earth in that moment. A picture of God for my mother's "God Box."

Cutting out the picture gave me a sense of purpose. Here was something I could do, a way I could help my mother. It wasn't hopeless. And then, Lauren walked in the door. She looked at the mess I had made on the floor. "What are you doing?" I collapsed in tears. "Jewell is dying."

* * * * * *

Lauren and I agreed we should go see my mother. The question was how to spring a surprise trip that involved Lauren without it seeming like we were coming because she was so sick. I did the only thing I could think of, I lied.

We had planned to go to the new Bellagio Hotel in Las Vegas for Thanksgiving, because, for us, nothing says "pilgrim" like a new hotel and casino. After we made our reservations, we happened to mention our plans to Jewell and she responded, "That sounds like fun. Maybe I'll come, too." So, we told her the trip was on us, made reservations for her at the hotel and reserved two extra seats for the Cirque du Soleil show.

Based on Julie's report of her condition, it was clear that she wasn't going to make it, so I decided to use that as a pretext for our trip to South Carolina. I told Jewell that, since she probably wasn't going to be able to come to Las Vegas, we wanted to come early to visit her and celebrate Thanksgiving. She said we didn't have to, we'd see if she was able to make it to the Bellagio. "Well, if you come to Vegas, that just means I get to see you twice," I said. "But you'll go [to Las Vegas] even if I can't make it?" Jewell asked. I assured her we would. Our gambling-filled holiday agreed upon, she said we could come to Greenville. She'd be happy to see us.

Questions I wish I'd asked my Mother • *Did she love Julie more than me as Julie claims?* •*Did my mother know I looked like an eggplant in my matching purple Danskin bellbottoms and turtleneck and, if so, why did she let me wear it?* •*What are we supposed to do with all of that fabric she had in her sewing room?* •*How mad was she when I had to go to the emergency room for alcohol-induced sunstroke during my college graduation?* •*If she could have changed anything about her life, what would it have been?* •*Why didn't she force me to wear dresses when I was a kid?* •*What was the most irritating thing about my father? My sister? Me?* •*Did she resent having to get up at 5:30 in the morning to take me to tennis lessons?* •*What was it like to grow up so far out in the country?* •*Under all that dye, what color was her hair?*

THE SEARCH FOR "MOMENTS"

One night, during the middle of the summer, I had this idea that I needed to buy my mother a watch. It seemed like a gift that would symbolize what we were going through, a way to commemorate the preciousness of time, the gift of life, etc. And, also, it would be expensive. I bought Jewell a lot of expensive gifts. She liked them because they were nice things she wouldn't normally buy herself and I liked them because they made me feel successful in her eyes.

With that psychological baggage in mind, I headed to a local store and spent an hour picking out the perfect watch. I tried on silver watches, gold watches, watches with leather bands and watches with metal bands. I finally settled on a Raymond Weil square-faced watch with a delicate linked band. It was beautiful. As I stood in the store looking at this watch on my wrist, I imaged the moment when I would give it to my mother. I imagined her reading my pithy card and opening the fancy Raymond Weil box. I imagined her trying on the watch and silently wondering, "How much did this cost?" The vision in my head was a perfect moment, one I would always remember.

I think there is a human tendency to seek out these "moments," experiences that resonate with profound meaning and emotion. I saw that watch as a memory in the making, a moment I would treasure forever.

Jewell didn't like the watch.

I think she appreciated the gesture and she seemed to be genuinely moved by my card, but she never wore the watch itself. She put it on after she opened it. But every other time I came to visit, she was wearing the ancient Seiko my father had given her many years before. My watch, my expensive "moment," stayed in the drawer.

* * * * * *

Mom and Dad weren't at the gate to greet us when Lauren and I arrived. Greenville has a small airport though, so I knew we'd run into them eventually if we headed toward baggage claim. As we rode down the escalator, I saw Jewell sitting alone by a sculpture in the lobby. She was wearing her light denim dress, the one she wore almost every day because it fit over her big belly.

> Journal, November 21 -- When we first encountered Jewell, I said, "Hey, you don't look bad" right after

greeting her. "Was I supposed to?" I realized I was verbalizing, perhaps inappropriately, my fears. The answer was "Yes, you were supposed to look bad. Julie told me you looked bad." What I said was "No. I just thought you would have lost more hair." Then I had to backpedal from that by saying, "Not that you look bad with no hair."

In truth, she didn't look as bad as I thought she would. Julie had alarmed me. June had sounded rational, but concerned. Jewell seemed weak (weaker than my last visit) and tired. Certainly more than I would want her to be. Not more than I'd expect from a cancer patient who had recently had pneumonia and a blood clot.

* * * * * *

Lauren is what I like to call "a delicate ecosystem." She is very sensitive and she likes being home with her foods and her friends and her things. As a result, she has a rule about travel. She never stays in anyone else's house for longer than two nights. If that means flying cross country for eight hours, sleeping, spending a day together, sleeping again and then waking up the next morning and leaving, so be it. It makes her trips easier. While Jewell was sick, I always visited my parents from Thursday to Sunday (three nights). I thought it was a nice trip, not too much flying for the length of the stay. Since Jewell was sick, I begged Lauren to bend her rule and stick to my travel routine. She reluctantly agreed.

Big mistake.

This trip was already fraught with a lot of emotional baggage, me pushing Lauren to do something she didn't want to do only made it worse. The afternoon we arrived, she began to feel guilty about missing the extra day of work and I got irritated that she couldn't let go of her guilt. That night, she couldn't sleep because of the time change. I taught her how to tell time by listening to the grandfather clock chiming outside the bedroom. All that did was help her to track how she wasn't sleeping in fifteen-minute increments.

During the day on Friday, she was a good sport with my mother. They lay on the bed together; they shared celebrity gossip and fashion tips; and they made fun of me, which my mother seemed to enjoy. By that evening, though, Lauren and I were fighting. As we got ready for bed, she told me she wished she hadn't violated her two-night rule. I countered with the incredibly mature "I wished I hadn't brought you at all." I cried. She cried. Finally, exhausted, I rolled over and went to sleep.

> Journal, November 21 -- At 5:15 a.m. she woke me up. "Girlie, I can't sleep." I woke up and she said she hadn't slept at all. She was so tired. She'd be tired today. She'd get sick. I immediately leapt into damage control. I apologized for all the things I'd said that night. It wasn't fair. It was all about my issues... She cried. The clock had been taunting her all night.

I finally got up and turned the chimes off.

* * * * * *

It was a strange weekend. We came to see Jewell before she died, but when we got there, she wasn't dying, at least not right in front of us. I had dragged Lauren cross-country for her "moment," some meaningful last words with my mother, but we weren't having that experience. The four of us were filling the days with activities: eating out, going to a show at the local community theater and driving to Asheville, North Carolina so we could introduce my parents to Lauren's mother and step-father. A lot of the time, we just sat at the kitchen table, talking. A lot of the talk was about cancer, but a lot of it wasn't. And everything that happened, everything we talked about, I filtered through the sense that, the week before, Jewell had looked bad enough that my sister thought I should fly right out to see her. But now, she seemed fine, or at least fine'ish.

> Journal, November 22 -- For the rest of the morning... all I could think was "this is the last time Lauren will probably see my mother." Just the idea of it made me sad. Lauren was great. She hung out with my mom. Ordered a fax machine on-line with my dad. And she didn't cry when we left. I asked her if she'd gotten to talk to my mom.
>
> "I gave up on that. I don't think that's what this trip was about."
>
> Dad took us to the airport. Before we left, he and Mom had a small skirmish about him going to Dillard's to buy a windbreaker. [As we drove away], she motioned to him... so he stopped the car and rolled down his window. "London Fog" was all she said. He rolled the window up and we drove away. Jewell stood in the door and waved.

This was the last time Lauren saw my mother alive. In the end, she got her "moment," her last words. They were "London Fog."

JOHN NEAL

That weekend, though, or maybe it was the weekend before when she looked so bad, was some sort of turning point. My mother began to talk more openly about how tired she was and the rest of us began to talk more openly about how afraid we were, even if we sometimes created problems where none existed.

> Journal, November 24 -- When I called this morning, Nettie [my parents' housekeeper] answered. My parents were at the doctor. Jewell was getting drained. I left a message.
>
> I hadn't heard by 5:00 their time, so I called back. My dad answered and said they'd gone to the doctor's office, but they hadn't been able to get any fluid out.
>
> "Really, what happened?"
> "I don't know. I wasn't in there. But when I walked into the room, your mother said 'tumor.'"
> "What do you mean, 'tumor'?"
> "I don't know. I wasn't there. I don't know if they saw something. Or if there is a large tumor growing. I didn't ask. I guess I didn't want to know.'

I told my father to have Jewell call the minute she woke up. "I'll ask the hard questions."

She called me in about an hour. Long enough for me to eat three chocolate covered fortune cookies.

"So, what's up?"
"We went to draw fluid. But they couldn't get any."
"Dad said something about a tumor…'
"Yes. They thought a tumor might be blocking the site they tried today. They have to keep moving around because the sites granulate."
"So there's no big growing tumor that's causing the swelling?"
"No."
"Will you do me a favor?"
"Sure."
"Go right now and smack Dad."

* * * * * *

My father doesn't seek out conflict or painful emotional experiences. It's not in his nature. He's always been a guy who wants or hopes or expects that things will work out and he'd rather just sit tight until that happens.

I remember once when I was in high school (back in the days before cell phones), we went to Ponderosa for dinner. After a delicious meal of thin steaks and greasy rolls, the four of us headed to the car. On the way, my father stopped at a pay phone to call a friend. Jewell, Julie and I stood about ten feet away and chatted amiably while he talked and, after a couple of minutes, John waved at us and said, "You go on." So, we climbed in the car and drove home.

Two hours later, my sister and I were playing basketball in the yard and we saw John turn the corner and head up the driveway. "Where have you been?" I asked innocently. My father, red faced and tight jawed replied, "Walking home from Ponderosa." My sister and I looked at him, dumbstruck. "You told us to 'go on.'" "I meant 'go on' to the car," he snapped. We laughed, apparently loud enough that my mother came outside to find out what was going on. Still laughing, we told her John's sad story. "Why didn't you call us?" She asked him. "Because I kept thinking it was a joke and you'd come back to get me." This only made my sister and I laugh harder. Jewell looked at him and shook her head. "If you don't have any more sense than that, then I'm not going to feel sorry for you." And she turned around and headed inside.

* * * * * *

My father took care of my mother every day while she was sick. All of the roles she had filled in their relationship for thirty-eight years, he took on. He ran errands. He filled prescriptions. He put meals on the table, even if the breakfasts came from Hardee's and the dinners from Swanson's. During one two-day stretch, my mother, trying to deal with her leaking fluid, sent him to the grocery store for Kotex and then for Depends. I tried to imagine my dad standing in the express line at Bi-Lo, a giant plastic package of Depends under his arm, oblivious to any thoughts of the people around him that he might be incontinent. John, just standing there, trying to think of what else he could do to deal with Jewell's draining.

I believe that my father suffered as much as my mother. He may not have had physical pain, but he lived through every one of her ups and downs. He lived with his helplessness and his fear. Every single day, he lived with cancer. Only, he didn't lose his hair or grow thin. There were no outward signs that he was suffering.

> Journal, December 14 -- Jewell got drained today. Dad said 7000 liters, then corrected himself. "That would be a lot of fluid." Apparently, they got as much out of that pocket as they could, but it didn't really decrease her volume all that much. Dad told me she had to sleep sitting up last night. She said she felt better [now].
>
> When I talked to Dad, he sounded sad and tired. I asked him why. And he tried to put me off with "No reason, really." Then, relented and said he was just "Tired and... down. About your mother, I guess. It's hard to watch her be that uncomfortable."

* * * * * *

Cancer is a lot like the Discovery Channel's Eco-Challenge. The Eco-Challenge is a strange race. A bunch of teams with funny names compete to see who can walk, climb, bike and kayak the fastest over a long course in a far off and inhospitable place. It's an endurance test. First of body, how much suffering can you physically stand? Then of mind, can you will your legs to keep moving even though your legs are telling you to stop? And finally of spirit. Some of the participants can't be stopped. With bleeding feet and sunburned skin, without sleep and sometimes far behind in the race, they keep going. And, in very similar situations, others don't. It's something deep inside them. Everybody has a point, a moment when they realize they have gone too far. They have endured too much. They hurt too much. The future seems too bleak. Or, maybe, stopping seems too wonderful. Who knows? But everybody has that point. The question is when do you get to it? And when you get to it, what do you do? What would Team Nash do?

WAITING FOR BABY JESUS

My mother loved Christmas. I don't know if it was because her birthday was on Christmas Eve, so it felt like her special day, or if it was all the extended family activities. Maybe it was the stuff. Gifts to buy, trees to decorate, folk art Santa Clauses to put out around the house, little snow villages to set out on the mantle. Whatever it was, my Mother devoted a lot of energy to Christmas. When they moved to Greenville, my mother started putting out two Christmas trees. One upstairs in the living room, another downstairs in the family room. The upstairs tree had our oldest ornaments on it, as well as the really good ornaments my mother had accumulated over the years. The downstairs tree, sort of a minor league decoration, I guess, got to hold everything else. They were both beautiful.

Wilma, Hilda and June had decorated the house last year, while Jewell was recovering from surgery and they came over to do it again this year. Jewell supervised, but didn't have the strength to participate. She hadn't had enough energy to make cookies either, or to wrap all of her packages. She even skipped buying a new Christmas sweater.

I love Christmas, too. It is a holiday I associate completely with my mother (my apologies to the baby Jesus). It is a holiday filled with rituals. My mom makes date balls for me and lemon squares for my sister. We take Jewell out for a fancy dinner on her birthday and go to the midnight service afterwards. On Christmas day, we open presents and, in the afternoon, go to a movie. We've seen some really bad movies on Christmas and always had a really good time doing it.

* * * * * *

My sister and I intentionally staggered our trips home. She was going early, so she would spend a few days with my parents alone. I was going to come a couple of days later and stay after she left. That way, my mom wouldn't have to deal with both of us leaving on the same day.

I was supposed to write a script for "Caroline in the City" while I was on Christmas vacation. The episode was about Caroline going home to Wisconsin for her parents anniversary party and discovering that they are selling the house she grew up in. The idea was loosely based on the trauma I had experienced when my parents announced to me that they were moving. (My mom told me they were moving after they had already bought a house in Greenville. They simply skipped the "thinking about moving" stage. I always felt lucky they told me they were leaving.) I had tried to get my writing assignment rescheduled, but it didn't work out. So, I had to write a half-hour comedy script while I sat at home with my cancer-ridden mother. It's not exactly the stuff great comedy is made out of.

> Journal, December 22 -- Julie arrived safely. And she says she thinks this is Jewell's last Christmas. Anticipating that, Jewell has apparently bought everyone very expensive gifts.
>
> Julie was driving mom around yesterday, running a few errands. They were using Julie's truck. It was so high that they had to borrow a stool at Wilma's for Jewell to step on in order to climb into the truck. When they were at Wilma's, Jewell was having a hard time getting her leg up the twelve inches required to step on the stool... Julie was trying to help her and Wilma was making suggestions. Jewell got so frustrated, she started crying.
>
> Julie said that Mom told her it is hard to fight back the "is this worth it" thoughts. Which must mean it's not worth it.
>
> Dad told Mom that if it had been legal, there were many times that he would have killed her, but now he can't imagine living without her.
>
> Suddenly, the prospect of going home and spending four days alone with my parents is very daunting. I can't imagine how those days will be filled. What will I talk to my father about? What will I do around the house? It seems like this endless void of despair that I'm going to be leaping into.

And I think about the future and the holidays seem even bleaker, just the three of us, desperately trying to make merry.

Now I'm supposed to work on my script and be funny. I don't feel like I have a funny bone in my body right now.

GRAY

My mom looked terrible.

> Journal, December 24 – I laid on her bed with [Jewell] tonight. [I asked if she was in pain.]
>
> "I don't have pain. I'm uncomfortable, with my legs and this big belly, but I don't really have pain... I don't think I'm going to go any time soon."
> "So we're probably okay waiting until tomorrow to open the gifts?"
> "Probably... I just don't know why this happened."
>
> How many times has she asked herself that question? It must be thousands, because she's asked me a couple hundred times and I'm not around that much. She seems to be tortured by that question. Every time she asks, I give the same answer, "there's no reason." She knows it intellectually; she doesn't know it emotionally.
>
> Maybe it's not important that she gets closure on that. Maybe I want too hard for her to find "peace" which of course, in my mind, means blind acceptance of the situation and moving on, whatever form that moving on takes (fighting, status quo, giving up).

There was an interesting aspect to my mother's decline. And, when I say "interesting," of course I mean "horrible." In person, until this visit at Christmas, I could never really see a difference in how she looked. Yes, I could tell if she'd gained a little weight. I noticed the things she pointed out to me. I saw the increasing number of scars on her abdomen from the draining procedures and the colostomy bags they stuck to her skin afterwards. I saw these things, but I couldn't "see" them. I couldn't look at the changes in her body and trace the course of her disease.

Now, after the fact, I can. If I pull out the photographs I took over these fourteen months, I can see her changing. She gets thinner, except for her belly which gets bigger by comparison. Her skin gets looser, hanging off her face like there is just too much of it. She also develops a gray'ish hue, as if she'd been standing still too long during a dust storm. It's impossible to miss, especially in the few black and white pictures that exist. If I lay the photographs on the floor and look at them, it's like a time lapsed movie. She dies right in front of you.

I couldn't see while it was happening, even though it was right there, hidden in plain sight.

On this visit, I finally saw it.

Questions I wish I'd asked my Mother • *How far did she actually walk to school as a child and did it really ever snow?* •*Who was the most influential person in her life?* •*What was the most embarrassing thing that ever happened to her?* •*If she could change one thing about herself, what would it be?* •*If she could change one thing about my father, what would it be?* •*If she could change one thing about Julie, what would it be?* •*If she could change one thing about me, what would it be?* •*What was her proudest moment?* •*Does she remember that really bad lamb lasagna she cooked in Wheaton?* •*How did she manage to plant her yard so that something was always blooming?* •*Why did she hate exercise?* •*Why did she buy so many clothes?*

THE FOOD NETWORK

Christmas Eve was my mother's sixty-second birthday. We did all the things we normally do on her birthday. We got up, got dressed and went to lunch. Jewell wore a black jumper with a white turtleneck. She pinned a small Santa to her dress. Her hair was thin, so she wore a floppy black hat to keep her head warm. She ordered crab cakes. Like always, I ordered the wine. Jewell ate a little of everything, not much of anything. When dessert came, Julie and I sang Jewell's birthday song. We made it up years ago, after the local grocery store, delightfully named "Jewel" started using a little jingle in their advertising campaign that went "Take a new look at an old friend, Jewel." For some reason, Julie and I had the inspiration to change it. For years, we have capped our Christmas Eve birthday celebrations with "Take a new look at an old mom, Jewell." She always seemed to like it.

When we came home from lunch, Jewell laid down for a nap. Julie started baking.

* * * * * *

My mother always did the cooking in our family. Julie and I weren't interested. When my mother got sick, Julie and I both started cooking. My efforts ran toward healthy, mostly vegetarian foods that my mother would claim to like and my father and sister would mock. Julie tried lots of things. She grilled. She broiled. She made soups. And on this Christmas holiday, she baked. She made me my date balls. She made peanut butter bars. She made Revel bars, an old family favorite. She tucked a dishtowel into her pants and baked, surrounded by a cloud of flour. My mother was astounded by this turn-of-events. She kept saying, "That Julie… will you look at Julie… Who knew that Julie…?" As if this fit of baking was the most magical thing she had ever seen.

While Julie was fulfilling this dream of my mother's, I was lying on the bed, snuggled up next to Jewell, watching the "Food Network."

* * * * * *

A couple of years before, my father bought a satellite dish. Jewell had resisted the technology back when it was first introduced because she thought giant satellite dishes sitting in people's yards were tacky. If something couldn't be disguised by hedges or azaleas, you had no right to make your neighbors look at it. Her resistance shrank in direct proportion to the size of the equipment. By the time they got down to eighteen inches, she couldn't come up with a good reason to deny my father this small pleasure. So, satellite television entered their world.

Initially, Jewell wanted nothing to do with it. She was perfectly content in her snowy three-channel broadcast world. She didn't see why she needed any more than that. And then, one day, my father found HGTV. As far as I could tell, HGTV was a collection of arts and crafts shows: people sewing little borders on tablecloths and making elaborate Christmas cookies. My mother loved it. She would put it on in the morning and watch it while she ate breakfast or turn it on while she made dinner. Since the house had only one satellite receiver, if Jewell watched HGTV in the kitchen, everyone in the house had to watch it, too, or resort to the three visible broadcast channels. It seemed every time you called the house and asked the question "What are you doing?" the answer was "Not much. Just sitting here, watching a little HGTV."

A few months later, my local cable television franchise added "The Food Network." I started watching it. Initially, I was addicted to "Taste," a simple little show which usually focused on one food item and various ways it might be used on its own or in recipes. I remember a particularly wonderful episode about honey. The host showed a short piece on honey collection and production and then did a taste test of various kinds of honey: clover, blueberry, tupelo. It was riveting, which is odd because I was watching a man eat something and then talk about it. It's a strangely removed experience I found captivating. I also watched "The Two Fat Ladies," a show produced by the BBC starring two overweight women who would cook pate in butter, stuff it inside a quail and then wrap the quail in bacon, something I would never eat but for some reason enjoyed watching them make. Another show starred a very large man who cooked food from the Mediterranean. And, of course, there was Emeril.

By the time my mother relapsed in June, I had introduced the whole Nash family to the "Food Network." We were addicted to "Emeril Live." The chef, Emeril Lagasse, has established a name for himself as the spokesman for Southern cooking in all of its forms. Now, most of its forms involve butter, pork or some other food I don't eat, but the show is still great. It's a lesson in the power of conviction. He's a true believer, so even if I don't agree that "Pork Fat Rules," I enjoyed his passion.

As my mother's health declined, her energy level waned and she was forced to spend more and more time in bed. So, the four of us would gather in my parents bedroom and watch the "Food Network" together. My sister and I would lay on the bed with my mother, me pressed tightly between the two of them. My father would sit on a chair by the bed. And we would all watch Emeril. We watched a lot. We watched so much that we would often tune in and discover that we had seen that evening's show before. "We've seen this," someone would say. "Really?" Someone else would answer. "It's the duck thing." "Oh, I remember. Emeril cuts the slits and cooks it skin side down. All that fat comes out." "Yeah, we definitely saw this." And then we would stay there and watch it anyway.

At the end of each episode, we would identify the recipes we had particularly liked and my father would be dispatched to collect them off the Internet. My mother kept a loose-leaf notebook of all the recipes she had collected from the "Food Network." I don't think she cooked a single one of them.

ALL IS CALM

On Christmas Eve evening, we went to church, the early service. Midnight seemed much too late for Jewell. My dad dropped my mother and me at the front door. I helped Jewell sit down in a pew toward the back. I sat on the end, next to my sister. My mom was next to her. My father sat on Jewell's other side. We all clutched the small white candles that the ushers had handed us on the way in.

It was a long service. There were a bunch of traditional Christmas songs, one song I'd never heard before and two sermons. Jim Nates, a kind and generous man, who was the senior pastor at Simpsonville Methodist Church, gave the first sermon. Jim had spent a lot of hours comforting my parents during Jewell's illness and I think we, as a family, felt a strong bond with him. The other sermon was given by the associate pastor. I don't remember what either sermon was about. I was too distracted by my fear that this was my mother's last Christmas. And I was sitting in church wondering if she was wondering if this was her last Christmas.

> December 24 -- We went to church. The service was nice. Long. 1 hour, 45 minutes. Lots of singing and Bible reading and a full sermon. I kept thinking about Jewell. I wonder if she sees everything through the prism of "is this my last..."? Because I do. We went up for communion. I was in front of mom. I took my bread and was moving off when I saw the assistant pastor…hand my mother a piece of bread and then reach out and touch her arm. It was an incredibly compassionate gesture. Full of love and sympathy. It made me cry. Fortunately, I had the whole walk up the aisle to compose myself. When we got seated again, I ended up next to Jewell. I held a hymnal for her. She has the worst singing voice, kind of off-tune and reedy, but she still sings. Not loud. Just loud enough for her to participate. And I thought, "Is this the last time?"
>
> The final song was "Silent Night." The whole lighting candles, five verses thing. I was holding my candle and the hymnal (for Mom and Dad). I started to tear up. Not bad, just enough that I couldn't see the words. I couldn't wipe my eyes (both hands occupied). I couldn't turn away. And I didn't want to cry in front of them. I don't want to be the sad, scared member of the family who drags everybody else out of denial. I looked to the front of the church. I willed myself not to cry. I took some deep breaths.
>
> I didn't cry, but I was trying so hard not to, that I missed hearing my mother sing those last two verses of "Silent Night." If that was her last Christmas, I gave part of it away. I wasn't looking at her. I wasn't listening to her. I was too busy trying not to feel. In retrospect, it doesn't seem like a particularly good choice.

The service ended. We blew out our candles and we went home.

> **Questions I wish I'd asked my Mother •**
> When did she know she was going to die?

REMEMBER ME

We always open Christmas presents the same way. We rotate. I'll open one, then my sister will open one, then my mother, then my father. Everyone gets a turn and everyone else watches that person open his or her present. There is a lot of "oohing" and "ahhing" over the stuff and this year was no different. After we had been through most of the gifts, my mother told us it was time to open our big gifts. She pointed to three items under the tree. She said they were all the same and that we had to open them at the same time. My father who already knew what it was, could man the video camera if that's what we girls wanted. So, on camera, my sister and I simultaneously opened our gifts. Julie, perhaps smarter than me or just having anticipated something emotional, stood behind my mother while she opened her package. I stood right in front of my mother. She watched as I ripped off the paper and snapped open the tape and pulled out her present.

It was a picture of her. It had been professionally taken. She was posed in front of a gray background. She was wearing a sea foam green top, her glasses held tightly in her right hand. She looked reasonably healthy. I mean, she had hair, short hair, but a fair amount of it. She was sitting behind a table, so I couldn't tell if her belly was big or not. As I looked at the picture, I wondered when she had it taken.

I heard her tell me that the photograph was taken "…by the man who had done our family picture. You know, the denim picture." I told her it was beautiful. I stared at it, still calculating time. Not too thin. With hair. Skin color okay. She must have done it before she went back on chemotherapy. After her relapse. While she still felt pretty good. August, maybe September. As I stared at it, she said, "That's the way I want you to remember me."

I moved in and hugged her so she couldn't see my expression. My sister was still standing behind her, carefully moving to the left and the right as Jewell turned around, trying to keep my mother from seeing her cry. I looked at my father. He was holding the video camera at arms length, pointing it toward me, his own picture of my mother clutched in his hand.

"That's the way I want you to remember me." Four months before, my mother had made an appointment to have her picture taken, anticipating that from that moment, she might never look or feel better. I was still stunned when I talked to Lauren later. "She had it taken four or five months ago. She knew." I said. There was a long pause and then Lauren replied, "Wow, she thinks of everything, doesn't she?"

* * * * * *

We spent the rest of Christmas day at my parents' lake house. For the last several years, my mother's close family has gathered there in the afternoon to exchange gifts and eat dinner. This year, except for my uncle Howard who had died the previous June, it was the same crowd as usual: Aunt Wilma, Aunt Hilda, Hilda's husband Howard, cousin Karen and her husband David, cousin Kathy and her husband Charley, Karen and Kathy's four children, and Aunt Brenda. Karen decorated the house. Everybody brought food. It was very festive.

> Journal, December 25 -- We got together with the Collins clan... and every time I was alone with someone, we talked about how Jewell was doing. Hilda cried at least four times. Karen cried at least once. Wilma cried at least once. Brenda cried twice, once about a recliner.
>
> Hilda told me when we were standing in the kitchen that she cries all the time. Driving, sitting at breakfast, taking a shower. That's how I feel. I wonder if her pain is different than my pain. Or if it's all just pain. The same ache in your core than you can't fix or cover...

* * * * * *

The Christmas before, Uncle Howard had dragged himself out of the house to be with us. He had some sort of blockage, so he couldn't eat. He just sat in a small recliner, an oxygen tank at his side, watching the festivities around him. This year, Jewell sat among us, eating her little bit of food, and wearing one of the two dresses she still fit into. She sat and she watched, as Christmas unfolded around her.

* * * * * *

My mother was always interested in things. Every morning of her life, she read the paper from front to back. She even read the "Metro" section; I have never met anyone else who reads the "Metro" section. She subscribed to a huge number of magazines: "Newsweek," "George," "People," "Country Home," and "Martha Stewart Living" to name just a few. She read every article and would save the issues that contained something particularly interesting. Jewell just wanted to know things.

And she loved to discuss the things she learned. For my whole life, being with my mother was like a talk show. She was the host and I was her favorite guest. Apropos of nothing, she would turn to me at breakfast and say, "Jan, what do you think of the new crime bill?" Now, my sister the police officer would seem to be the perfect person to ask about this, but Jewell never did. She always asked me. She wanted my opinions and, to be perfectly honest, it bugged me. I should have been flattered, but I wasn't. I was annoyed. Her questions pushed some sort of giant psychological button. I would dismiss them, answering in a cursory fashion or, sometimes, not at all. These were not my finest moments.

> <u>Journal, December 25</u> -- I look at Jewell and, honestly, I don't see my mother. It's not just that her face is thin and her hair is falling out. It's the way her mouth moves and her eyes. I remember my mother laughing and talking. This woman is quiet.
>
> There was a moment in the car today when I felt as if we had gone back in time. Jewell asked me "what I thought was going to happen to Bill Clinton." In so many different moments, I have been irritated by questions like that. Today, I launched into a long-winded answer to the question. I didn't really care, but I seemed like I cared. Jewell didn't say much… but she was there, listening. Being my mother. Caring about things I don't care about.
>
> That's what I'm going to remember. My mother wants to hear what I have to say about everything. My mother thinks I'm smart and successful and can do anything I set my mind to. And she's really proud of herself for having raised me.
>
> That's what I want to remember. The woman who cheered me at games. Got me out of school to go shopping. Let me go around the world by myself. Got over her prejudices and self-recriminations about my lifestyle and embraced the person I love. Laughed at my jokes. Told me that I was "destined for greatness" at a moment in time when I had no idea what that meant. And then told me I was everything she every wanted when she was wheeled off for her first surgery.
>
> My mother believes in me. And she loves me. And she's leaving.

WALKING AND WAITING

At some point during my early research, I had read that exercise was important for people with cancer. It helped with their energy levels. It helped with their responses to chemotherapy. It helped their appetites. It just helped. So, when Jewell was first sick, I used to ask her to walk with me around the circular driveway in front of my parents' house. It was only a tenth of a mile, but even a little bit of exercise, I figured, was better than none. She almost always agreed. My mother listened to me about things like that, even if she didn't believe it herself.

Recently, though, I had stopped asking. It just seemed too hard. She didn't enjoy it and the slow deliberate pace we moved at depressed me. Where was the vigorous, fast mall-walking mother I knew? On the day after Christmas, Jewell asked me to take a walk around the driveway with her, as if volunteering for exercise proved that she was still committed to her own recovery.

Journal, December 26 -- Jewell put her purse down and said, "Let's try to walk around"... We'd finished about a quarter turn, when Jewell started to get emotional.

"This is just so hard... I'm tired of having no energy and I don't want..." She stopped.
"You don't want what?"
"I don't want for this to get worse, to think that I'm only going to have less energy. And I don't want to die young."

I didn't say anything. I can't say she's not going to die or that she shouldn't worry. I can't offer her supportive platitudes that I don't mean. I just held her hand on my arm and was silent.

"Your father wants me to come out here and do this every day. But I don't see what difference it makes."

Jewell went inside and laid down. After awhile, I went in and joined her.

"You know, Mom. Walking around that loop might not make you feel physically better, but at least you'll be outside under a blue sky. Maybe that will make you feel emotionally better. And if you still don't want to go out there and walk around, then fuck it. Do what you want."

She laughed.

* * * * * *

This was, I think, the first time I answered my mother's pain and her confusion with silence. I couldn't tell her that what she feared – that things would get worse, that she was going to die – weren't going to come true, because I knew, in my heart, that they were. My mother was going to die of ovarian cancer, probably soon. I could no longer pray for her to recover, or even for her to hang on and be with us for another few months. I began to pray that she would not suffer.

* * * * * *

Journal, December 27 -- My father watches my mother. I know that because I watch her, too, and I see him staring at her. Sometimes she's asleep. Sometimes she's awake. He just looks at her. There's no real expression on his face. He doesn't look sad. But I wonder what's going through his mind.

This morning, I woke up and ate breakfast. We weren't going to church. My mom had decided to sleep in. I walked into their bedroom later and found them watching live broadcast from the Spartanburg Baptist Church. I sat down. A few minutes later, my father got up and went to get Julie. She came in and sat down. We were at church together, even though we were sitting in my parents' bedroom. During the "Lord's Prayer," I looked over and my mom had her eyes closed and she was mouthing the words. Even the "Amen." She wasn't talking loudly. I couldn't hear her. I just watched her lips move.

After the sermon, Julie walked quickly by me toward her room. She was crying. I followed her asking, "Are you okay?" She said she'd be fine. I asked what was wrong and she gave back the answer I used last time we were together: "I don't know if you heard, but my mom has cancer." It made her laugh, at least. She wondered if she should stay longer. Is this going to be the last time she'd see Mom alive?

"No. Well, I don't know. God didn't tell me, or I'd mark it on the calendar so we could all relax... or not. But I don't think so." I tried to tell her that, even if it was, she needed to keep her life going. "What if it's not? Are you going to hang around until April?"

[Julie] has the same fears and feelings we all do. It's why Dad watches [Jewell]. Because he knows she's leaving.

Tonight, we watched more cooking shows. I went outside for a little while to watch the stars. When I came back in, we watched more cooking shows. Julie showed us her "stick a Kleenex up your nose" technique for combating her spontaneous bursts of running snot. Mom ate a tangerine. I ate an orange.

HEAVEN

Julie left early the next morning. She was driving home and wanted to get an early start. My father woke me as Julie was packing her truck. It was pitch black outside. I headed toward the front door and found my mother sitting in the entry hall. She was wearing a blue, fuzzy-looking nightshirt, her plump feet encased in dark socks. Her hair, the little bit of it she still had, was matted down. She was sitting straight up in the chair, like she had been called to attention. The front door was open. Jewell was just staring outside, watching Julie and John carry bags to the truck and throw them inside.

Finally, the truck was packed and my sister came back in to say goodbye. Jewell stood up and hugged her. I heard her say, "I love you. You have no idea how much." And then, after a moment, Julie headed out the door. As she walked down the front sidewalk, she turned and waved at us and my mother, from her perch on the chair, waved back.

I videotaped this whole exchange. I don't know why. Somehow it seemed like something we should have. Did I want to look at it? I didn't think so. Maybe my sister would. The last moment? Who knew? But, unfortunately, it was dark in the hall and, on the film, people move in and out of shadows. The picture quality is poor. The only part that really turned out is the first image: my mother sitting on her chair, all alone in the hallway, staring out the open front door.

* * * * * *

After my sister left, the mood around the house was somber. My mother spent most of the day sleeping, leaving the rest of the family to deal with their very complicated feelings about what was happening. My sister called from the road and told me she felt liked she'd run out too fast. "I should have taken more time," she said. "Just in case."

>Journal, December 28 -- This morning, Dad sat down at the kitchen table with me and started crying.
>
>"I just wish there was something I could do."
>"You're doing as much as you can. You're doing everything we, or Mom, could expect."
>"I just wish I could take away her pain."
>"I know you do. But you can't. You can do laundry. You can help her off the toilet. You can't take her pain away."

So, we were all worrying and wondering what to do. Karen thought we should talk to the doctors about ending Jewell's chemotherapy, since it seemed to be wearing her down and perhaps causing more harm than providing a benefit. I told her I couldn't do it. If Jewell wanted to stop, I would support her, but I wasn't going to initiate the discussion.

I felt helpless. If we were having these feelings, then Jewell must be having these feelings.

* * * * * *

And then, just when I felt the most lost, I found my moment of grace.

> Journal, December 28 -- I put Jewell in bed tonight. I changed her dressing and got the covers arranged. Then I leaned on her side and said, "You know, you can tell me anything... I don't want you to feel alone."
>
> She told me to lay on the bed. I did. I curled up next to her and we talked.
>
> She told me about her funeral. She has clothes picked out. She hopes they fit. She wants a memorial service and then to be buried at Nash Grove. [Jewell started crying.] We were just laying there, silent. And then she said, "Will I recognize Julia in heaven?"

It's such an abstract concept, heaven. What is it? How does it work? Newsmagazines do stories about the afterlife all the time. People dying in the middle of surgery, floating above the table, walking into a white light, seeing the faces of people they knew.

I believe in heaven. I'm not sure exactly what it looks like, but I believe in a space where people go and experience the all-consuming love of God. Or call it the Universe. Or call it your own essence. It doesn't matter to me what you call it. I know it's there. And I knew, in that moment, my mother was going to go there. She clearly didn't remember asking about her parents, Paul and Julia, after her surgeries. She didn't know, as I knew, that she had seen them already. Right then, my mother, who has always just wanted to love and be loved, feared being alone for all eternity. "Will I recognize Julia in heaven?" She asked. And God gave me the strength to talk to my mother's fear rather than dismissing it. "Of course you will," I said. "She'll be waving and shouting 'Jewell, over here.' You'll know right where she is. And you can, as Lauren likes to say, hold hands and frolic in the meadow." Jewell looked me in the eyes and smiled. "That sounds like fun."

> Journal, December 28 -- Jewell told me about a small red
> box that's in her stuff. It contains a barrette of mine from
> childhood and a triangle of money. Her Grandmother
> Pelfrey had left money in a bank during the crash. She
> been advised to take it out, but she said she trusted the
> bank. It crashed, but, years later, the bank made good on
> the losses. Uncle Reid made a claim. When they divided
> it up among all the children and heirs, Julia got $2.47

(that's what mom remembers). Julia gave it to Jewell and told her it was her "inheritance." Mom told me it was mine.

She told me that Julie and I were fine young women, and that she was very proud of us.

I asked her if she would come and visit after she died (though I don't think I used the word "died"). She said she would. She told me that Julia comes to her sometimes. She doesn't talk, though. She's just around.

"Has she been around since you got sick?"
"No."
"I bet she has."
"Maybe. I've probably just been too self-absorbed to notice."
"Not self-absorbed. Medicated. You're not particularly self-absorbed."

She asked me if I had any questions, medical or otherwise. I said "no." The only thing I cared about was knowing what we could do to end her discomfort. And for the rest, "I want to know whatever you want to tell me. Your stories. The objects that have value for you. I'm just sorry that I waited so long to start listening."

"Yes, we waited too long."

She told me that she was going to give my sister $5000 when she got her house.
"Your father knows to give you an extra $5000 later. And between the life insurance and my investments, there should be $10-15,000. You get yourself something you want."
"I can't have what I want."
"I know. But buy something that will help you remember."

When she was talking about her funeral, she said "Your father will be at wit's end, but he'll be okay."

"I know he will. We'll take care of Dad."

I asked her if she was angry about laying in the bed all day.

"Angry? No."
"Then how do you feel about it?"
"Like it's a waste."

I told her I wanted to be like her when I grew up. She told me I would.

She fell asleep lying there on her side. As she breathed, she made little puffing sounds. I watched her for awhile and then I got up and went to bed.

* * * * * *

How do you say goodbye to someone you love? I don't know. I never said goodbye. But on this one evening, I did the next best thing. I was there for my mother. I didn't run away from her pain. I didn't run from my pain. I was there, lying on the bed with my mother, promising her that she wouldn't be alone in heaven.

> Journal, December 28 -- I worked a little bit today. I felt singularly uninspired. I felt like my brain was lead. I wasn't having any funny ideas. Or really any ideas. All I want to do is watch Jewell. I know how John feels.
>
> She laid down for the entire day. She ate half a piece of cheese toast, one-third of bowl of gumbo and some pasta. She drank some water and a cup of chamomile (she calls it "camille." I don't correct her) tea. She smacks her lips constantly. I think she's always dry. The edges of her

teeth are turning brown. Her hair is thinning. When she wakes up from a nap, it's all wet like a baby's.

It rained today. I never got outside.

THE LENGTH OF EVERYTHING

Jewell had chemotherapy on December 29th. My father and I drove her to the doctor's office in the morning. We waited with her until a nurse took her to the back to hook her up to the IV bags that were her chemotherapy and nausea drugs and her fluids. Apparently, fluids are really important. You need to pee; otherwise all these drugs just sit in your organs and kill you instead of the cancer.

John and I ran errands and then stopped to get Jewell some lunch. We brought it back and discovered they had moved her. Her abdomen was so huge, they decided to drain her. She was in a private exam area. We found her lying on a table, chemo drugs being injected in one arm, ascites fluid draining from the giant needle in her abdomen into bag hanging below the table, and a Foley catheter inserted up her urethra so she wouldn't have to get up in the middle of all this to go to the bathroom.

Dr. Puls, Jewell's oncologist arrived just as we pulled out her lunch. My father went out into the hall to talk to him. I tried to listen to their conversation while talking to my mother at the same time. I asked my mother how her sandwich was while I listened to Dr. Puls tell my father that Jewell produced more ascites fluid than any of the other five hundred ovarian cancer patients he had treated. Jewell and I discussed whether the giant needle in her abdomen hurt while Dr. Puls reiterated that my mother's comfort was the most important thing to him. Jewell told me she was tired as Dr. Puls tried to reassure my father about how hard my mother was fighting and how, even at this point, Dr. Puls was hopeful that they would get results from the chemotherapy. My father came into the room. Jewell said, "I heard you talking to the doctor. What did he say?" My father paused and then told her that Dr. Puls was still hopeful that Jewell would have a good response to chemo.

Just then, I flashed back to a similar moment I had several months before. Julie and I had accompanied Jewell to chemo and, after we escorted her back to the room where they administered it, we had run into Dr. Puls. We asked him how Jewell was doing and he launched into a long discussion about her course of treatment and the difficulty of dealing with the ascites fluid. In the middle of it, almost casually, he said, "… the outcome's not in doubt. The cancer will win…" I remember standing there, stunned, thinking, "He just told me my mother is going to die." I couldn't focus on anything else he said. Later, when Jewell asked Julie and I what the doctor had said, the two of us exchanged a look before quickly saying, "He told us you're doing great." Now, I wondered if that little white lie that I told to shield her from the pain of a terminal disease helped her. Or if it even helped me.

* * * * * *

The night before I left, my mother hemmed the chef's pants I had gotten for Christmas. I had gotten chef's pants because I'd asked for them. I thought they looked cool on the Food Network. The pair I got were four inches too long and, the night before I left, Jewell said she would hem them for me. I told her she didn't have to, but she insisted. So, I washed and dried them, put them on and stood on a chair so she could fold up the extra material. She sat at the kitchen table, in her usual seat, cutting off the extra material, marking the bottom with a sewing pencil, pinning the hem and, then, carefully sewing the new hem in place. It took her forever. She moved slowly, deliberately. I watched her the whole time. She didn't talk much. She just sewed, until both legs were done. She handed the pants to me. I pronounced them perfect. It was the last motherly thing Jewell did for me. I haven't worn the pants yet, I'm too afraid something will happen to them.

Questions I wish I'd asked my Mother •*What does she remember from my childhood?* •*What does she remember from Julie's childhood?* •*Why did she keep so many unlabeled packages in the freezer?* •*How did she feel when my father was fighting in Korea and Vietnam?* •*Why was she obsessed with celebrities?* •*How did she learn to walk into ugly houses and see their potential?* •*Did she like any of the tofu recipes I made for her, or was she just being polite?*

MOTHERS AND DAUGHTERS

We got up early the next morning. Jewell had to go to the doctor's office before they closed for New Year's Eve. We planned on going to breakfast afterwards and then my father would take me to the airport.

> Journal, January 1 -- Yesterday, I left South Carolina and came home. We had a nice morning. My mom had been draining all night. Dad said they'd changed the bag at 1:30 and again at 5:30 a.m. We changed it again before we left for the doctor's office. She needed to get there in the morning for her Neupogen shot. As we were driving over, she said, "I think I'm going to let you get me a wheelchair." [Her] famous, "I'm going to let you... I'll have to tell you..." as if all of the decisions of life are dictated my some outside force.
>
> The wheelchair didn't have footpads, so at one point, Dad said she was shuffling her feet on the ground, trying to keep them from being wheeled under the chair.
>
> After the doctor's office, we went to the Waffle House for breakfast. It was a happening place. We were waited on by a woman who calls herself "grandma." We marveled at the short order cook who seemed to be able to keep all

of the orders in his head. We debated how many Waffle Houses there were in the USA (2000, according to grandma) and in South Carolina (probably 500). We enjoyed our waffles and cheese sandwiches and then we went home.

Dad emptied Jewell's bag and I brushed my teeth. When I went into their bedroom, Jewell was sitting in the chair. I asked her what she was doing. She said she was going to take a nap.

"Should I take your shoes off?"
"Oh, I think I can get it."
"I don't mind."
"No, I'll be okay... well, go ahead, you do it." I did.
"It's a shame when you can't do things like that for yourself."

She patted her lap. I sat down.

"You take care of yourself while I'm gone."
"I'll be fine. Don't fret."
"I don't fret. I just want you to be okay."
"I am okay."
"Or as okay as you can be, right?"
"Yeah. I guess that's it."
"I love you."
"And I love you. You have no idea how much I love you."

It is hard to find the words for that last moment at the door. I had hugged her and kissed her and told her I loved her and, still, it didn't seem enough. Leaving seemed too hard. But I had to go. As I stepped outside, she held the door open and I turned to look at her and she looked better, in that moment, than she had looked in a long time. She was smiling and, even with her thinning hair and skinny face, she looked like my mother. I said, "Hold on," dug my camera out of my bag and pointed it at her.

If you look closely at the picture, you can see me reflected in my mother's glasses. Me pointing a camera at her. Her smiling. The picture turned out great. It was the last time I saw my mother alive. And I have a picture of it.

* * * * * *

When I was in the fifth grade, I had to do a leaf project. I was supposed to collect leaves and tape them to a piece of poster board, identify what kind of tree they were from and give a few facts about those trees. Most of my collecting was of a "find a leaf on the ground and pick it up" variety, but we had a redbud tree in our backyard that refused to shed any of its precious foliage.

It was a sad little tree. At some point before we moved into our house, it was struck by lightening. The bolt had ripped through the middle of the tree trunk, creating a giant hollowed out cleft. The tree was mostly dead, but each spring, one branch continued to bloom, bright pink buds and tiny green leaves. In the interests of science, I decided to climb up the dead center of that redbud. I got to the one live limb and reached out to grab a leaf. As I stretched out my hand, I lost my balance and fell, right arm first, ten feet to the ground.

I picked myself up and ran into the house to find my mother. Since she was a nurse, she was exactly the kind of woman you wanted to go to when you thought your right arm was about to fall off. I opened the back door to the kitchen. Jewell was sitting at the table, sharing a cup of coffee with one of her friends. I clutched my right arm to my chest and, through heaving sobs, told my mother that I had fallen out of the tree onto my arm. When I had finished, Jewell looked at me a moment and said, "Well, that will teach you to be more careful, won't it?" Then she calmly turned back toward her friend and continued her conversation.

I remember standing there, confused. It wasn't the reaction I expected. But, I immediately realized I <u>was</u> okay. After a minute, I stopped sniffling, released my arm from its death grip at my chest and went back outside to continue my project.

* * * * * *

This is my favorite story about my mother. I told it all the time, to any friend of mine or friend of my mother's that would listen. Jewell thought I told it to make her look bad. But, I don't think she looks bad. I mean, somehow she knew I was okay. And instead of upbraiding me for risking bodily harm by climbing a dead tree, she just told me to be more careful the next time I decided to do something foolish. She was giving me a life lesson: "Shit happens." Of course, that's not something my mother would have said to a ten-year-old.

Questions I wish I'd asked my Mother •*What were all those "things" she was going to show me?*

THE END

Jewell went to my Aunt Wilma's for New Year's Day. Everyone was there. They ate collard greens and black-eyed peas. When I called, they were having a wonderful time. Jewell said she was eating, but reported that her stomach was a little upset. She was still sick two days later.

> <u>Journal, January 3</u> -- Jewell is still sick... Dad says she sleeps and suddenly wakes up, trying to vomit. Since there's nothing in her stomach, it's mostly dry heaves. She had a small fever yesterday (about 100.4). Today she's normal.
>
> I asked him what he thought was wrong. He said what is in the back of everyone's mind.
>
> "Well, everyone wonders if it might be an obstruction. Which would be bad, because that's serious. Hopefully, she just picked up a virus. Charlie had a virus. Hopefully, she'll feel better tomorrow."
>
> I remember the conversation Julie and I had with Dr. Puls about how most ovarian cancer patients die of bowel obstructions. Or, more accurately, they waste away

because of their bowel obstructions. And since that day, I have waited for the arrival of the dreaded bowel obstruction.

A little information is a bad thing. All I know is bowel obstruction. Now, all I can think of is bowel obstruction.

I've been calling home two times a day, hoping that the second call will bring the news that Jewell is feeling better. So far, that hasn't happened. I'm just hearing twice a day that she's not feeling well.

* * * * * *

My father took my mother to the doctor on Monday, January 4th for her regular visit. A nurse tried to take Jewell's blood pressure. She didn't have one. Well, everyone has one; hers was just so low it was hard to measure. They admitted her to the hospital.

They wheeled her from the doctor's office to Room 681, the room she had been in for every one of her other hospital stays.

> Journal, January 4 -- I was driving to work today, enjoying my new Jack Kornfield tape, almost without a care. He was talking about impermanence and I was really thinking about how I could implement that idea in my own life.
>
> When I walked into the office, [one of the assistants] started walking toward me with great purpose. My father had called. It was some sort of emergency. He left his cell phone number.
>
> I called Lauren before I called my father. I thought maybe he would have talked to her and told her the news and it would be easier to hear from Lauren than from my

dad. He hadn't told her anything. She said he was crying.

I called Dad. He had taken Jewell to the doctor's this morning for her Neupogen shot. The nurses thought her nausea was caused by dehydration, so they were going to give her some fluids. When they took her blood pressure it was 70/40 something, almost immeasurable. They couldn't get a vein for an IV, so they admitted her to the hospital. They were waiting for a doctor to come and put in a central line. Doctor Hunter had asked my father if my mother should be coded in the event of an emergency.

"What did you say?"
"I told him that your mother wouldn't want to be a vegetable."

Several hours later, he asked me if I agreed with his decision.

I asked him if he's called Julie. He said he had tried her, but hadn't connected. At first, he asked me to call, but then he retracted the request. He would try her again. I asked if I should come to Greenville. He said we should wait an hour before deciding. Let the doctor come and do the central line and tell us what was up.

"I just don't know." He started to cry.
"Dad, everything is going to be okay. No matter what happens. I know you can't believe that now, but I know it's so. Everything is going to be okay. I promise."
"I don't know. I just don't think so."

I called about every half-hour. For the first several hours, there wasn't much news. June and Tom had come to keep my dad company. No one had come to put in her line. Jewell was restless and incoherent. The nurses had finally managed to get enough blood out of her neck to do her lab work.

At one point, a surgical resident came by to try and do her central line. He didn't feel confident in his ability to do it, so he left it for a more senior doctor.

Hilda showed up.

The lab results come back. [But no one could find them.] A real doctor comes to put in her [central] line. They took an x-ray. A resident was looking for the x-ray. When they found it, they would know if the line was in the right place. Then they could start the fluids. After six hours in the hospital, they still hadn't started her fluids. Her blood pressure ticked up a few beats. June said that it was at a normal level. "Mine could be that if I was laying down."

Finally, the fluids got started. They had changed what they gave her because her lab results indicated that her electrolytes were all out of balance. The line was bothering Jewell, she kept scratching at it.

Dad asked Dr. Hunter if I should come back. He told John that he doesn't make predictions, but that his plan was for my mother to go home in a couple of days. Dad told me to wait and see how things were in the morning.

Jewell was restless. Flopping from one side to the other on the bed. Squirming around, laying in the bed sideways. Sidling up to the bed rail and then throwing her arm over the side of the bed. They gave her some Ativan, but it didn't seem to help.

"Did you ask if they would give her some more?"
"Yes, a while ago."
"Then go out to the nurses station and stand there until someone gets a syringe. A squeaking wheel gets the grease."

When I called back, he had gotten Jewell more Ativan, but she was still awake and still agitated. The nurses might give her 5 mg more if she needed it.

During the day, Jewell has been mostly delirious. Early in the morning I called and she seemed alert. Dad handed her the phone and I talked to her.

"You're being very dramatic, Mom."
"I don't mean to be, honey."
"I love you."
"I love you, too."

If she died tonight, I would know that the last thing I said to her was "I love you." But I suspect that would be little consolation in my pain.

Any notions I had of implementing "impermanence" in my life have vanished. I know that this is a better moment for my mother to slip away than when she is dissipated and weak, but I'm still not ready to say "goodbye."

Jewell slipped in and out of coherence during the day. She said, "I was awake," "I think so" and "Angela's teaching now" to no one in particular. Someone came to take her EKG and she asked what they were measuring for. At one point, she asked my Aunt Hilda how far she was from Minneapolis, St. Paul and turned to my father and said "Honey, help me." He asked what she wanted and she replied "Shrimp." My cousin Karen had an Indian friend named Asouk, who worked in the hospital pharmacy. He came to see how Jewell was doing and she called him "Jan."

My father said she kept pulling her gown off. They would put it on again, only to have her immediately rip it off. After awhile, they just let her lie in bed naked. My Aunt June arrived wearing a brightly colored jacket, which my mother immediately grabbed and put on. She was sitting in bed, completely naked under this jacket. She spent five minutes trying to button it, even though it had no buttons.

I didn't go to South Carolina. I waited in L.A. for someone to call me and tell me something.

> Journal, January 5 -- The phone rang at about 12:40. Lauren dropped it on the floor. When we finally found it, Julie was on the line. My dad had changed his mind. He wanted me to come home on the first flight. Jewell's breathing was labored. According to Julie, he thought she was going to die. I hung up with Julie and called USAir. I was dismayed when they told me the 8:20 flight was sold out. The earliest I could get out was 9:00, and I'd have to connect through Pittsburgh at a cost of $750 each way. I could get the emergency fare if I waited until 11:40 p.m. and took the red eye.
>
> I asked which other airlines serviced Greenville and the woman told me Delta and Northwest. I hung up, crossed to the bedroom to tell Lauren I couldn't get a flight, and waited for a reservations agent to answer Delta's phone. One did. I said, "I need to fly to Greenville, SC for a medical emergency, can you tell me what's available?" At that moment, call waiting went off. "Can you hold for a minute?" I asked. "My other line is ringing." I clicked over and it was Julie. She didn't say "Hello."
>
> "There's no easy was to say this…"
> "She's dead."
> "She's dead."

This is another one of those moments I have replayed over in my mind a thousand times. It is always the same. My sister says, "There's no easy way to say this." I interrupt her with "She's dead." And Julie matter-of-factly responds, "She's dead." It's not an emotional conversation. They're just facts, relayed between two people who know that they are true.

> Journal, January 5 -- I was standing in the doorway to the bedroom and I remember saying "She's dead." Lauren took the phone out of my hand. She talked to Julie a moment. I kept mumbling "Delta's on the other line."
>
> Lauren asked Julie to call back and clicked over to Delta. The woman had waited. She helped Lauren get me a reservation at 7:15, arriving in Greenville at 4:40 p.m. Lauren hung up.
>
> I was in a daze. Lauren suggested that we lay on the bed for a minute. So we did. We held hands and talked about the end of Jewell's suffering, how chemo had done her a favor by killing her, etc. And then Lauren cried. I held her. I didn't really cry myself.
>
> After a few minutes, I decided I needed to call Dad. I dialed the hospital's main number, explained that my mother had died and asked to be connected to my father. I was. A man answered the phone.
>
> "Hi, this is Jan Nash. I'm calling to talk to my father. If he wants to talk."
> "I'm sure he will."
>
> After a minute, Dad got on the phone. He said that Jewell had been restless all day. Late in the evening, her breathing had gotten labored. He was holding her hand and could feel how much she was struggling. He went

and got a nurse, who listened to mom's lungs and said they sounded "dirty." A doctor was called. They were in the process of doing a chest x-ray when she stopped breathing. The doctor came and asked my father if he wanted my mother put on a respirator. Dad said "No."

Lauren made an interesting observation tonight. The first was that, after a lifetime of being fascinated by "stuff," my mother never took the time for us to go through hers. Lauren thinks that maybe it just wasn't that important to her at the end. It was just stuff. The other observation was that, despite how much my father wanted my mother to stay around, in her final moment, he let her go. He didn't ask the doctor to try and save her. He let her go. It was a brave and selfless act.

Wilma called while we were packing... She was calling to see how I was. She shares my feeling that this may be best for Jewell; it's not best for us. It must be so hard for her. Two painful losses in the same year... Wilma said that Hilda told her that Jewell kept saying, "I'm going to die. I'm going to die." Wilma's response to that was, "She may be." And she was. I wonder if her agitation today was aimed at letting go, or holding on. I told Lauren that I thought she was moving around because "she had someplace to be." And now she's there...

Julie called right as we were leaving for the airport. They wanted me to write the obituary. I don't know what to write. I always think of obituaries as dry, factual things. And, the facts of my mother's life, how can I reduce all she was to those simple elements?

"Jewell Geneva Nash, loving wife and mother, sister and friend, made the transition from life to more life on January 5, 1999. She was a good woman with a wonderful sense of humor. She threw great parties."

My aunt June told me that the day before she died, Jewell turned to her and said she had a big day planned for tomorrow. "What are you doing?" June asked. "I'm going to the mall," my mother replied. Jewell loved shopping. I guess that was her idea of heaven.

> Journal, January 5 -- I remember back when we first got Jewell's diagnosis. Ovarian cancer. We ran home and searched the Internet for news. We found it, mostly of a sad and dispiriting variety. It was a horrible cancer with lower than average survival rates. In those moments, I believe I lived through my fears of this day. Would she die? And, if so, how soon? Will she suffer? When, when, when, when, when? Ultimately, all of my "guesses" (which were probably just my hopes disguised as something else) were wrong. At every step of the way, nature or fate or God has defied us. The disease proceeded at its own pace and in it's own way.
>
> And now, the day has finally come. Jewell is dead. I can't hardly believe it.
>
> Lauren believes that God wanted Jewell from the beginning. All these complications were his way of getting her home faster. But Jewell wasn't ready, so she fought and she held on and she stayed. For fourteen glorious months. Until finally, she couldn't fight it any longer.

TAKING IT WITH YOU

My father found the brand new outfit Jewell picked out for her own funeral. It was a bright print, lots of greens, pinks and blues. For some reason, she hadn't chosen any jewelry, so John asked everyone which earrings he should send to the funeral home. Julie and I finally convinced him just to pick the ones he liked best. He also sent the Seiko watch he had given Jewell years before and, after asking me if it was okay, the Peretti Bean necklace Lauren and I had given her for Christmas two years before. "I know it was expensive," he said. I told him it didn't matter. He should do what he felt was right.

John, Julie and I went to the funeral home before the visitation, so we could spend some time alone with Jewell. I hadn't decided if I was going to look at her. I'm not a fan of the embalmed dead body. I've only looked at two of them and I haven't been able to shake either image out of my head. I didn't want my last image of my mother to be of a waxy-looking corpse. Julie volunteered to go look at the body for me and gauge whether she thought I'd be okay. She walked over to the casket, looked, came back and told me that, while Jewell didn't look completely like herself, she didn't look bad. Julie thought I could handle it. I decided to look, mostly because I didn't want to be left out while Julie and my father looked. We were a new family and I wanted to be included in our first family activity. It's not a good reason, but it's the real reason.

Julie was right. Jewell didn't look bad. She just looked dead. Her arthritic hands were really thin. Her face looked pinched. Her lips were all wrong. But, she didn't look bad. In fact, for the first time in fourteen months, she didn't look pregnant. All of the fluid had been drained from her abdomen. She was small enough to wear her new outfit. Jewell had great taste. The bright print worked.

* * * * * *

My mother grew to loathe the denim dress she wore almost every day. It was one of only two outfits she had that fit over her big belly. She told my dad that when she got better, she was going to burn it. So, after the visitation at the funeral home, we went back to the house and did just that. She was finally better, so we opened some champagne, raised our glasses and toasted Jewell, as the hated dress disappeared, consumed by flames in the fireplace.

THE LONG GOODBYE

I don't think I'll ever get used to the idea that Jewell is dead. I described it to someone as being like a glass sitting on a table. The glass sits in one place. Every day, you walk by and look at that glass, sitting on that table until you don't think about it anymore. It's just a glass on a table. One day, without you knowing how it happened, the glass moves to the other side of the table. It's disconcerting. It's still a glass on a table, but something about it isn't quite right. It will never be right. Yet, that's the way it is.

* * * * * *

I learned a lot as my mother died, all of which I would give up if I could have her back healthy and happy. But, I know I can't, so I'll keep my lessons and try to turn them into something positive.

First and foremost, I learned what a horrible disease cancer can be. It steals the lives of its victims, one little bit at a time. It attacks the body, the mind, and the soul. It is a painful process to watch and, I imagine, even worse to experience. But, as an exit strategy, I think it has advantages over car crashes and heart attacks and things that kill people instantly. Mostly, it is the advantage of time. Time to learn how to die or, in my case, how to let someone die. I never quite got it right. I tried. But, in most moments, my need to have my mother in my life, overwhelmed my good intentions. I wish I could have so many of those moments back. The moments when I told her she was going to be okay or that she would have good days. I was offering false hope. She knew it. I knew it.

I should point out that this is my experience of my mother's cancer. Every situation is different. One of my aunts and my oldest friend have both undergone successful cancer treatments. They are cancer survivors. In those two situations, hope was justified. And, even in my mother's case, as long as she had hope, I believe I was compelled to support her in that optimism. I just took it too far, trying to hold on to a rosy view of the future when Jewell was ready to see the world differently. She was isolated and alone. Who was left for her to share her fears with?

I don't blame myself for these deficiencies. I did the best I could. Hopefully my best today is a little better than my best back then.

The second thing I learned and, this will sound heartless, is that the fear of my mother dying was much worse than her actually dying. Once it happened, it was over. It wasn't "out there" anymore, a big unknown thing we couldn't imagine. Once she died, we didn't have to imagine it. It was a fact. We cried. We mourned. We bound ourselves together in our suffering and then we moved forward. It started almost immediately. My Aunt Wilma called me less than an hour after my mother died. She reached out to me, offering maternal comfort. She stepped in and tried to fill, in whatever way she could, the void that Jewell's death had created.

And, finally, I learned that writing about my mother, talking about her, praying about her -- basically any type of communication either shared or solitary -- eased my pain. In the months after she died, all I could remember was a thin, balding woman, living her life as best she could. Thinking and talking about her life and death has put cancer into its proper perspective. These were just fourteen months in the course of sixty-two years. They were a part of my mother's life; they did not define my mother's life. As I wrote this book, she transformed back into the woman I knew before cancer. In my mind's eye, she has hair. She can eat whatever she wants. She wears stylish clothes. She loves to shop. She throws a party and everyone comes. And in the center of it, she stands, laughing. Jewell is alive.

* * * * * *

Ultimately, death was not the enemy. My fear of death was the enemy. Death was a gift that released my mother from suffering.

A SHORT HELLO

My mother told me that, after she died, she would visit me on my birthday. On February 16th, I waited, but she didn't come. Or, if she did, I was in such an agitated state, I couldn't feel her. Not too long after my birthday, though, I had a dream. In it, I was talking to some friends from college. I was telling them about my mother's illness, how sick she was. Just then, someone behind me said, "Jan, your mother is here." I turned around and there she was. Only, it wasn't my mother as I had last seen her and as I was describing her to my friends in the dream. She was healthy. Her face was pink and round (forgive me, Mom, for calling you round). Her hair was full, frosted with lots of curls. I stood there, stunned, because in my mind, in that moment of the dream, I knew Jewell was dead. She smiled at me, stretched out her arms and said, "I come all this way and you're not even going to give me a hug?" I couldn't move. She walked over and wrapped her arms around me. I immediately woke up. The first thought that popped into my head was "… came all this way? Does that mean Greenville, SC or heaven?" When I woke up the next morning, I knew the answer was heaven. My mother came to visit me and let me know she was okay.

* * * * * *

Julie told me that she wasn't afraid of dying anymore; because now she knows she'll get to see Jewell. And she's right. Jewell will be there. As I walk into the white light, her voice, with its soft, lyrical southern accent, will call me forward. "Jan, honey. I'm right over here." She'll have made dinner. Fried chicken, mashed potatoes, maybe fried okra or corn, and, of course my favorite, strawberry pie. We'll sit down to eat and the two of us will pick up right where we left off.

> ***One Final Question I Wish I Could Ask My Mother•*** *What did Julia say when she got to heaven?*

AN UPDATE (AND THANKS)

I was changed by the experience of my mother's death and the changes continued. Lauren and I broke up. We weren't making each other happy, but managed to keep an iron grip on our relationship for a long time anyway. Jewell dying, realizing the role fear played in my experience of her death, helped me see that while change is never easy sometimes it is necessary. Now, the struggle of holding that relationship together has been replaced by the ease of loving someone else. I have a home filled with people and dogs. Joy has, in a word, multiplied. (Lauren is not, by the way, her real name. I don't know enough about how she is now or what her life has become to impose our shared history upon her.)

My father was lucky enough to find a "new wife" and she's terrific. My Mom shouldn't have worried about the stuff. Melinda wanted us to have it.

Thanks to Liz and Abe; John and Julie; Sarah, Heather, Wilma, Hilda, Karen, Kathy, Brenda, Yair, Susan, Suzanne, Brad, Michael, Kathleen and all the others who held my hand through these days and the many that followed.

And, of course, Jewell, who was there in spirit.

Made in the USA
Lexington, KY
27 November 2009